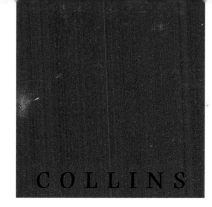

COLLINS

gardening for birds

COLLINS

gardening
for birds

Stephen Moss

Illustrated by Gill Tomblin

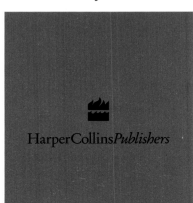

HarperCollins*Publishers*

HarperCollins*Publishers*
77–85 Fulham Palace Road
Hammersmith
London
W6 8JB

The HarperCollins website address is:
www.**fire**and**water**.com

Collins is a registered trademark of HarperCollins*Publishers*

Originally published in Hardback 2000
This paperback edition first published 2001

2 4 6 8 7 5 3 1

02 04 05 03 01

ISBN 0 00 712317 5

For Sally and John Rose

Acknowledgements
I would particularly like to thank Chris Harbard and Mike Everett at the RSPB, Derek Toomer
and Andrew Cannon at the BTO, and Chris Whittles at CJ Wildbird Foods for their expert help and
advice during the preparation of this book. Thanks too to Katie Piper, Claire Marsden, Myles Archibald
and Jenny MacMillan at HarperCollins, for their expertise and encouragement, and Gill Tomblin for
her delightful illustrations. My family have, as ever, been supportive during a difficult time for all of us.
And finally, thanks to Suzanne, for opening my eyes to the joys of garden birds – and so much more.

Garden illustrations by Gill Tomblin
Flower artwork from *New Generation Guide Wild Flowers*
Bird artwork by Norman Arlott

Front cover photograph of Great Spotted Woodpecker © Mike Wilkes/Aquila Photographic
Back cover photograph © Garden Picture Library

Designed by Rod Teasdale
Colour reproduction by Colourscan
Printed and bound by Rotolito Lombarda SpA, Milan, Italy

Contents

Gardens for Birds

With a little work, care and attention and a good dose of imagination, any type of garden, however small, can be transformed into a haven for birds and give both its owners and the birds that visit it the maximum amount of benefits and enjoyment. Knowing which species are likely to be attracted to your particular garden and location, and taking advantage of the opportunities for increasing the numbers and types of birds that visit it is the key to successful gardening for birds. The following chapter looks at six different kinds of garden and describes the ways in which you can encourage and care for the birdlife in them.

▲ THE TERRACE ROOF GARDEN pages 8–13

Don't be deterred by a lack of space: this section shows you how to allow birds to get the most out of the smallest, and seemingly most unpromising urban 'garden' and tells you which species are likely to benefit

▼ THE SMALL SUBURBAN GARDEN pages 14–17

The best ways to maximise space for birds in a small suburban garden and encourage them to nest, roost and feed there, as well as what species to look out for depending on the location of your garden

▲ THE URBAN GARDEN pages 8–13

However tiny the patch of green you own, learn to provide a birdlife sanctuary in the heart of the city that will attract a variety of town-dwelling species as well as many other kinds of birds passing overhead

▶ THE LARGE SUBURBAN
GARDEN pages 18–21

Transform a garden in the leafy suburbs into a welcoming environment for birds, and make the most of the opportunities for increasing the range and numbers of common and less frequent rural species that visit it

◀ THE COUNTRY
GARDEN pages 22–25

A larger country garden can offer a range of mini-habitats for different species of birds. Find out how in addition to the common garden birds, you can attract scarcer, more localised species to a rural garden

▶ UNUSUAL GARDENS pages 26–29

Whether you own a croft on a remote Hebridean island or a coastal garden on the Isles of Scilly, this section gives useful practical advice to those with more 'unusual' gardens and tells you which species to look out and care for in different regions of the country

7

The Terrace Roof Garden

*Not everyone is lucky enough to have a garden,
particularly if you live in the centre of a town or
city. However, if you have a roof terrace or even
a balcony you can still entice the birdlife that
exists around you. House Sparrows may drink
from birdbaths or water feeders, pigeons may
take a rest from their endless search for scraps
and Carrion Crows are always on the lookout for
extra food. Tower blocks that rise high above
street level can be a good vantage point for
watching urban birds and even those with simply
a window sill can attach bird feeders to windows
and place water containers or window boxes
outside which can provide a welcome resting
place for birds.*

The Urban Garden

In the heart of the city, a few tiny oases of green remain, visible only to the Kestrel as she hovers stock-still overhead, her piercing eyes scanning the ground below for the slightest motion. There is a tiny movement, and in an instant the falcon's wings fold and she plunges to the earth below, seizing the unwary rodent in her sharp claws, before flying up to a convenient perch on a nearby window ledge. Meanwhile House Sparrows squabble for scraps of bread, constantly chirping as they jostle each other for position. You may see Starlings digging their sharp beaks into the green baize lawn; and everywhere, the gentle cooing of dozens of Feral Pigeons provides a chorus to the day's events.

The Urban Garden

LIFE IN THE CITY

You might think that town and city centres offer little in the way of attraction to birds – but you'd be wrong. Millions of people means tonnes of food: dropped accidentally by the busy commuter, offered casually by the office worker enjoying a lunchtime sandwich in the park, or given deliberately by the urban householder who knows the birds need all the help they can get.

City birds, like the people who live there, are streetwise: clever crows, always on the lookout for an opportunity to snatch a scrap to eat; gaudy Magpies, their machine-gun rattle calling their comrades to rich pickings; and of course those troublesome pigeons, or, as many an exasperated Londoner has been heard to call them, 'rats with wings'.

New birds are moving into the city, too; they may visit gardens or be seen flying overhead. Mallards raise chicks inside the central quadrangles of high-rise office blocks. Gulls – once mostly Black-headed but now also marine species such as Herring and Lesser Black-backed – build their nests on warehouse roofs and raid gardens for food. Even Sparrowhawks and Peregrines – once driven to the edge of extinction by the indiscriminate use of pesticides – are now returning to our city centres.

It's not all good news, though. The House Sparrow – the fabled 'cockney sparrer' of legend – has become an increasingly rare sight in our towns and cities. Song Thrushes once sang on every street corner; in some cities they are now almost as rare as nine bob notes. Even Blackbirds are beginning to fall in numbers. The causes of these declines are far from clear, but they mean that the dawn chorus struggles even more than usual to overcome the noise of the traffic.

THINGS TO CONSIDER

More than anywhere, in the city size and space are your main consideration. Be realistic regarding what you can achieve, but don't limit your ambition too much – you'll be surprised at the number of different birds that can and do turn up, given time!

A full scale bird table may be too big for some city-centre gardens. If that is the case, maximise space by using the largest hanging feeders, which allow half a dozen or more birds to feed at the same time. Peanuts and seeds, as always, are the staple diet and should attract a few tits and finches as well as the usual sparrows and starlings.

Urban birds can't afford to be fussy, so kitchen scraps are always welcome, and may attract larger birds such as crows and gulls. Watch out, though, that you don't play host to

SUITABLE EQUIPMENT

■ at least two, preferably more, seed and peanut feeders, ideally the largest ones available to make the best use of space. These can be hung from a bush or shrub, or if you're really pushed for space, one model has rubber suckers so it can be stuck onto the outside of a window-pane!

■ a birdbath, however small and simple, will allow birds to take a drink; a larger one allows them to bathe too.

■ if you have the room, put up a nest-box; perhaps an open-fronted one for Robins, or a 'tit-box' for Blue Tits or (with a slightly larger hole) House Sparrows. More than one nestbox may cause territorial disputes in a small garden, so use your judgement when choosing a site for them.

ABOVE: *A clean, fresh supply of water is as essential for the birds in your garden as food*

RIGHT: *Even the smallest urban garden will accommodate one or two seed feeders*

less welcome visitors such as mice or rats, which can become real pests.

Water is often at a premium in city centres, so a regularly filled birdbath is essential. Nestboxes may be a luxury you feel you don't need, but try putting one up – you might be pleasantly surprised!

PLANTS TO GROW

Your best bet is to choose hardy, adaptable shrubs and bushes that maximise the amount of cover for the birds to roost and build their nests. You may prefer non-native plants, which tend to do well in cities, but if you can, choose at least one or two native varieties, as they are more likely to attract the few insects that are still around.

Climbing plants such as honeysuckle offer plenty of food and cover in a limited space. You may also be able to plant a flowerbed or two, which can be stocked with a wild flower mix to make them more attractive to butterflies and other insects. And if space is really at a premium, don't forget hanging baskets; they are often a favourite nesting place for Robins!

Climbing honeysuckle (bottom) or a gooseberry shrub (centre) provides cover for roosting or nesting birds, while wild flowers, such as daisy (top), attract insects and other invertebrates

WHAT WILL YOU SEE?

Even the smallest urban garden will attract the standard range of city-dwelling species, while many others may pass overhead and be attracted down into the garden from time to time to feed. If you are lucky enough to live near a park, all sorts of other birds may turn up.

RESIDENT (PRESENT THROUGHOUT THE YEAR):
■ Kestrel, Feral Pigeon, Wood Pigeon, Pied Wagtail, Wren, Dunnock, Robin, Blackbird, Song Thrush, Blue Tit, Great Tit, Magpie, Carrion Crow, Starling, House Sparrow

SPRING AND SUMMER VISITORS:
■ House Martin (late April to September), Swift (early May to July)

Robin

AUTUMN AND WINTER VISITORS:
■ Black-headed Gull, other gulls (including Common, Herring and Lesser Black-backed) Long-tailed Tit

OTHER POSSIBLE SPECIES:
■ Sparrowhawk (especially in gardens near parkland), Jay, Redwing, (occasional in autumn and winter), Mistle Thrush, Chaffinch, Greenfinch

Redwing

The Small Suburban Garden

As dawn breaks, the Robin is usually the first bird to end
the night's silence. His song wakes the early commuters:
an unwelcome signal to leave the warmth of their beds
and get ready for work. The sound also acts as a
signal to other songbirds, and soon a Blackbird,
Song Thrush and Wren have joined the
chorus. As the grey February light begins
to filter through to the streets below,
finches and sparrows come to feed,
while a pair of Collared Doves coo to
each other on the garden
fence.

The Small Suburban Garden

HAVEN FOR BIRDS

Like the railways, suburbia is a 19th-century invention; and like the railways, it changed our lives forever. At first those little plots of land, hemmed in by roads and houses, were identical. But gradually, as each proud homeowner sought to make a statement of individuality, the suburban garden was born. The result: not the bland sameness that makes up so much of our modern landscape, but a proud patchwork quilt of colour.

Despite their small size – some only a few metres square – Britain's suburban gardens have become a haven for birds. Some species, such as Collared Dove, Wren and Dunnock, spend the majority of their lives there. Others, like Starling and Black-headed Gull, spend much of their time elsewhere, feeding on nearby school playing fields or in local parks. But they are always quick to return,

Above: *Make room for at least one or two nestboxes for hole-nesting species such as Blue and Great Tits*

to take advantage of a free lunch.

Many species are only occasional visitors to the small suburban garden, depending very much on the location.

For example, if your garden is anywhere near a small wood, you may be lucky enough to get a visit from species such as Coal Tit or Great Spotted Woodpecker; while if you live by a park you should hear the deep loud rattle of Mistle Thrushes flying overhead.

But whatever the location of your garden you need to maximise the range of facilities you provide. As with an urban garden, space is at a premium, and the birds will have to compete with the needs and requirements of many other creatures – including, of course, yourself.

THINGS TO CONSIDER

In most small suburban gardens, size and space is very limited. Remember that you or your family will want to use the garden for recreational purposes, so it may be sensible to limit the amount of space you give over to birds.

It's a good idea to have a single, compact feeding station, such as a bird table with hanging feeders, serving a limited variety of key foods including peanuts and seeds. Keeping things simple has the added advantage that you'll be able to maintain a well-stocked and clean feeding area.

Remember that suburban birds can be just as hungry as rural ones, and will empty your feeders very quickly, so consider what you can afford before you decide on the number and range of feeders.

However small your garden, there should also be space to provide at least one nestbox away from the feeding area, for hole-nesting species such as Blue or Great Tits. You may not have quite enough room for a garden pond, but a small birdbath takes up very little space, and is an attractive garden ornament as well.

If you lead a busy life, try to keep maintenance to a minimum, by

SUITABLE EQUIPMENT

■ a bird table – either hanging from a wall or fence, or mounted on a bracket or post – is essential. It allows you to provide a variety of food in a limited area, keeping the rest of the garden free for other activities such as nesting or bathing.

■ simple seed and peanut feeders can be hung from the table itself, or from a nearby bush or tree; squirrel-proof feeders are essential in most suburban gardens.

■ a birdbath is an attractive feature, allowing birds to drink and bathe regularly. Water is just as important as food.

■ one or two standard nestboxes should be provided, but make sure they aren't too close together or you may end up with territorial disputes.

■ small gardens aren't suitable for most specialised nestboxes, but if you have a House Martin colony nearby, try putting up a specially-designed box for this charming summer visitor. Pied Wagtail and Wren may also nest in specially-designed boxes.

planting perennial shrubs and bushes that need little or no pruning. Letting a small part of the garden 'go wild' may make life easier for you as well as helping the birds, but remember that your neighbours might not be quite so overjoyed if the weeds end up on their neat lawn! Thick cover also provides a roosting and nesting place for many different species, and enables them to hide from predators.

Cats are a particular problem in the suburbs: it's often hard to discover where they come from and who owns them, and many a suburban gardener has resorted to guerilla tactics to rid themselves of this feline menace. Wild predators such as grey squirrels, rats and mice are also a constant hazard.

The good news, however, is that even the smallest suburban garden should, with careful planning, attract a wide variety of birds – with the bonus that you can often observe their behaviour at very close quarters indeed!

PLANTS TO GROW

Space is at a premium in most small suburban gardens, but even so it's worth having at least one reasonably large shrub or bush. The birds may use it to nest or roost, or simply as a place to perch while waiting their turn at the feeding station.

Suitably hardy native shrubs include crab apple, elder and hawthorn, while non-native barberry and forsythia are popular with gardeners as well as with birds. Leyland cypresses may grow too quickly for a small garden, but are particularly favoured by thrushes and Greenfinches, and are also easy to grow and maintain.

If you have walls and fences, try planting climbers such as honeysuckle and ivy, while if you have a 'wild garden', teasel and brambles provide an excellent food supply for birds such as Goldfinch and Song Thrush.

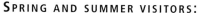

WHAT WILL YOU SEE?

As with any garden, the range of species you attract will depend on your geographical location and immediate surroundings. Some of these birds can be found in almost every suburban garden; others may be scarce or localised, or only occasional visitors.

RESIDENT (PRESENT THROUGHOUT THE YEAR):
■ Sparrowhawk, Feral Pigeon, Wood Pigeon, Collared Dove, Pied Wagtail, Wren, Dunnock, Robin, Blackbird, Song Thrush, Blue Tit, Great Tit, Jay, Magpie, Carrion Crow (Hooded in north-west Scotland and Ireland), Starling, House Sparrow, Chaffinch, Greenfinch

SPRING AND SUMMER VISITORS:
■ House Martin (late April to September), Swift (early May to July or August) Goldfinch (spring)

AUTUMN AND WINTER VISITORS:
■ Black-headed Gull, Redwing (especially in hard winter weather), Mistle Thrush, Long-tailed Tit, Coal Tit

Greenfinch

Wood Pigeon

Mistle Thrush

OTHER POSSIBLE SPECIES:
■ Rose-ringed Parakeet (London suburbs), Great Spotted Woodpecker (near woodland), Blackcap (mainly autumn and winter), Goldcrest (mainly autumn and winter), Siskin (mainly winter)

Barberry

Dense shrubs or bushes offer a place for birds to nest or roost, and may have the added benefit of bearing nutritious berries

Bramble

Dog rose

The Large Suburban Garden

Mid-May, and as the sun begins to set, hordes of House Martins twitter in the darkening sky, snatching tiny insects from the air as they go. Flocks of Swifts chase each other like fighter planes, giving the piercing scream which earned them the folk-name of 'Devil bird'. A month ago they were heading north from their African wintering grounds; now they are at their summer homes in the leafy heart of suburbia. On the roofs of the well-spaced houses, Blackbirds and Song Thrushes continue to sing, despite the fact that the breeding season is now well underway. The distant yaffling call of the Green Woodpecker dies away, while from the nearby park, a Blackcap pours his song into the evening air.

The Large Suburban Garden

UNDER AN ENGLISH HEAVEN

England is full of gardens like this: proud patches of green in the leafier suburbs, on the edge of our towns and cities. Middle England, the newspapers call it, and this applies to the birds as much as anything else.

Most of the species found in urban and small suburban gardens are here, of course, often in greater numbers than before. But they are also joined by a few of their rural counterparts: woodpeckers and warblers, owls and Jackdaws, visitors from the countryside who take advantage of the healthy supplies of food to be found nearby.

Depending on the garden's proximity to woodland, you are likely to hear the song of three of our commonest warblers, Willow, Chiffchaff and Blackcap, to get visits from one or two species of woodpecker, and to enjoy winter invasions by scarcer finches such as Siskin.

Even so, there are some species, such as Yellowhammer and Turtle Dove, which you would consider yourself lucky to find in the suburbs,

Above: *Install a birdbath large enough to allow birds to bathe as well as take a drink*

and whose current scarcity makes them less likely than ever to stray here.

THINGS TO CONSIDER

Space is unlikely to be much of a problem in most large suburban gardens, although as always, the amount you give over to the birds will vary depending on the needs and requirements of you and your family.

Start by finding the best place for the bird table: not too near the back of the house, as this may put off the shyer species, but not so far away that you cannot enjoy the view! You may prefer to install one of the 'space-age' designs of feeding station featured in the catalogues of the specialist bird food retailers, but even if you do, a traditional bird table is always a good idea too.

Plenty of feeders – containing peanuts and a variety of different seeds – are also essential. Try unusual seed mixes such as nyger (or niger), for Goldfinches and experiment with different coloured feeders.

A birdbath, placed some distance away from your feeders to avoid contamination, is another essential piece of equipment, while a pond, however small, will always attract a greater variety of birds to your garden.

Most large suburban gardens can support at least three, perhaps more, nestboxes, as long as they are strategically placed to prevent raiding by predators. Try varying the size of the hole to attract Great Tits and Nuthatches as well as Blue Tits. An open-fronted box may even attract Spotted Flycatchers if you are very lucky!

PLANTS TO GROW

Hopefully you will already have one or two large, mature trees. If not, don't worry; native bushes such as hawthorn or elder are almost as effective at attracting birds, and grow a lot more quickly! Evergreens such as cypresses grow even more rapidly,

SUITABLE EQUIPMENT

■ as in any garden large enough, a bird table is essential.

■ you should be able to provide a good range of seed and peanut feeders, including squirrel-proof ones!

■ at least one birdbath, perhaps two if you have the room.

■ two or more nestboxes should be provided, with a variety of entrance sizes and designs.

■ you may also want to try putting up more specialised nestboxes, depending on the species seen regularly in your garden.

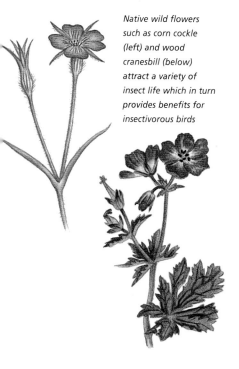

Native wild flowers such as corn cockle (left) and wood cranesbill (below) attract a variety of insect life which in turn provides benefits for insectivorous birds

WHAT WILL YOU SEE?

Like its smaller suburban counterpart, this garden should attract a reasonable cross section of species, though this will of course vary depending on where you are in the country and whether you have parkland, woodland or farmland nearby.

RESIDENT (PRESENT THROUGHOUT THE YEAR):
■ Sparrowhawk, Feral Pigeon, Wood Pigeon, Collared Dove, Green and Great Spotted Woodpeckers, Pied Wagtail, Wren, Dunnock, Robin, Blackbird, Song Thrush, Mistle Thrush, Long-tailed Tit, Coal Tit, Blue Tit, Great Tit, Nuthatch, Jay, Magpie, Jackdaw, Carrion Crow (Hooded in north-west Scotland and Ireland), Starling, House Sparrow, Chaffinch, Greenfinch, Goldfinch

SPRING AND SUMMER VISITORS:
■ Swift, House Martin, Swallow, Blackcap, Willow Warbler, Chiffchaff, Spotted Flycatcher

AUTUMN AND WINTER VISITORS:
■ Black-headed Gull, Common Gull, Fieldfare, Redwing, Blackcap (from central European population), Siskin, Reed Bunting

OTHER POSSIBLE SPECIES:
■ Grey Heron, Buzzard (western and northern Britain), Kestrel, Pheasant, Stock Dove, Tawny Owl, Rose-ringed Parakeet (London suburbs only), Lesser Spotted Woodpecker (England and Wales), Goldcrest, Marsh Tit, Treecreeper, Bullfinch

and are excellent nesting and roosting sites for Greenfinch, Goldcrest, thrushes, pigeons and doves.

If your house faces in a southerly or westerly direction, it may be ideal for climbing plants such as honeysuckle or even wisteria. Walls facing north or east are better suited to ivy, which produces plenty of berries as well as providing dense cover for nesting Wrens and other species.

By early summer, your flowerbeds should be a riot of colour, with a good variety of native wild flowers attracting butterflies, which in turn lay eggs and produce caterpillars to feed hungry young Blue Tits.

And don't neglect your lawn; many species such as Pied Wagtails, Starlings and Blackbirds enjoy feeding on an open lawn. If you have enough room, why not give over some space to a 'wild garden', with seed-bearing plants such as teasel – ideal for Goldfinches in late summer and autumn.

Chiffchaff (top left), Fieldfare (right) and Buzzard (bottom left)

The Country Garden

A frosty January afternoon, with the sun peeking from behind grey clouds. On the wide open spaces of the lawn, a Green Woodpecker forages for ants. Meanwhile, its tiny Lesser Spotted cousin creeps around the branches of a beech tree, searching for small insects. On the bird table, Marsh and Coal Tits join their commoner relatives, while Bramblings and Tree Sparrows hop about on the ground below, picking up spilt seed.

The Country Garden

RURAL IDYLL

Take a walk in parts of Britain's countryside today, and you'll be lucky to hear a bird sing. That's because modern farming methods have turned much of lowland Britain into a sterile monoculture of wheat or barley, virtually devoid of birdlife.

In contrast, a well-managed rural garden may support a wide variety of scarce and common birds which puts the surrounding countryside to shame. It offers a wide range of mini-habitats, with fragments of mature woodland, open lawns, shrubs and bushy areas, all of which provide a variety of places for birds to feed, roost and nest.

As in towns and suburbs, the commonest birds are typical garden species such as tits, finches and thrushes. What's different is that you may get visits from scarcer, more localised species as well as the

Above: *Take advantage of the space available in a country garden by providing a large feeding station that will serve a variety of species*

common ones. Other birds are almost exclusively confined to rural areas, as they depend on large areas of traditionally-managed woodland or farmland to survive. These include resident species such as Pheasant, Barn and Little Owls and Rook, as well as summer migrants like Turtle Dove and Garden Warbler.

Many rural gardens need relatively little work to turn them into magnets for birds, although continued maintenance can be time-consuming, especially if you have a large garden.

THINGS TO CONSIDER

Depending on the location and amount of space available, a country garden can provide the ideal opportunity to create a near perfect 'service station' for birds. As with most wildlife gardening, the secret is to avoid over-management, and if you can, to let a substantial part of the garden 'grow wild'.

Your only problem with feeding is likely to be the amount of money you need to spend to keep up with your hungry customers! As always, one or more bird tables are essential, while with feeders, the sky is the limit. Simple nut and seed dispensers are fine, but if your budget can stretch this far, you can purchase feeders costing more than £100, which dispense a variety of gourmet foodstuffs and can support up to a dozen birds at a time.

The best nesting sites are natural ones such as holes or crevices in trees, but if these are in short supply you can provide a wide range of standard and specialised nestboxes. The standard variety will soon be occupied by tits or sparrows, while specialised versions include those for Kestrel, Barn Owl or Treecreeper.

A garden pond is essential if you want to attract water-loving birds such as Grey Heron and Kingfisher,

SUITABLE EQUIPMENT

■ at least one, preferably two, bird tables, suitably positioned to allow birds to approach from a variety of directions and perches, while close enough to the house to enable you to watch them.

■ a large feeding station so that a variety of species can feed without too much competition. Try varying the amount and range of food until you achieve the right balance.

■ at least one birdbath – though if you can, a small bath for drinking and a larger one for bathing will help smaller species get their turn more quickly.

■ a garden pond, ideally surrounded by a damp, marshy area planted with native wild flowers.

■ a wildlife area, perhaps including a miniature 'hay-meadow', and a variety of seed-bearing plants.

■ a variety of standard and specialised nestboxes.

PLANTS TO GROW

With luck, your garden will already have several mature native trees such as oak or ash, birch or beech. If you are near a river, alders are perfect for attracting finches such as Siskin and Redpoll, and willow trees also attract a wide variety of feeding birds.

Planting trees may seem a long-term investment, but apple and hawthorn grow quickly, and are useful for birds after only a few years. Large flowering shrubs such as berberis and cotoneaster provide juicy and nutritious berries, ideal for winter thrushes such as Fieldfare or Redwing – or if you are exceptionally lucky, a flock of Waxwings.

Climbing plants such as honeysuckle and ivy are also excellent for providing food and cover, as well as being attractive in their own right.

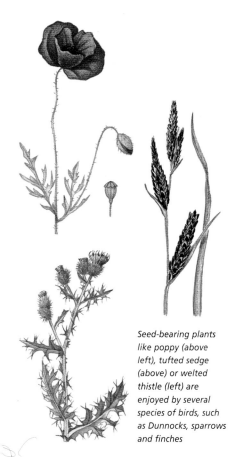

Seed-bearing plants like poppy (above left), tufted sedge (above) or welted thistle (left) are enjoyed by several species of birds, such as Dunnocks, sparrows and finches

while a marsh area around the pond creates an excellent habitat for native plants and insects, which in turn will attract a variety of insectivorous birds, especially during the spring and summer.

As well as the usual garden pests and predators, you are likely to attract foxes, hedgehogs and even badgers, all drawn to your garden by the prospect of a free meal. This isn't necessarily a problem, as long as there's plenty of room for the different creatures to co-exist. Nevertheless, regular cleaning of feeders and the clearing up of waste food is essential if your garden is to remain a sanctuary for birds.

WHAT WILL YOU SEE?

The composition of species will be determined by your location and immediate surroundings, and by changes in your local environment.

RESIDENT (PRESENT THROUGHOUT THE YEAR):
■ Grey Heron, Sparrowhawk, Kestrel, Stock Dove, Wood Pigeon, Tawny Owl, Green and Great Spotted Woodpeckers, Pied Wagtail, Wren, Dunnock, Robin, Blackbird, Song Thrush, Mistle Thrush, Goldcrest, Long-tailed, Marsh, Coal, Blue and Great Tits, Nuthatch, Treecreeper, Jay, Magpie, Jackdaw, Rook, Carrion Crow (Hooded in north-west Scotland and Ireland), Starling, House and Tree Sparrows, Chaffinch, Greenfinch, Goldfinch, Linnet, Bullfinch

SPRING AND SUMMER VISITORS:
■ Turtle Dove, Cuckoo, Swift, House Martin, Swallow, Garden Warbler, Blackcap, Willow Warbler, Chiffchaff, Spotted Flycatcher

AUTUMN AND WINTER VISITORS:
■ Fieldfare, Redwing, Blackcap (from central European population), Brambling, Siskin, Redpoll, Reed Bunting, Yellowhammer

OTHER POSSIBLE SPECIES:
■ Buzzard (western and northern Britain), Pheasant, Barn Owl, Little Owl (southern Britain), Lesser Spotted Woodpecker (England and Wales), Waxwing (winter visitor, mainly to eastern Britain), Grey Wagtail, Hawfinch

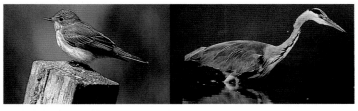

Spotted Flycatcher (left) and Grey Heron (right)

Unusual Gardens

Spring comes early to the Isles of Scilly, and on sunny days in March the Parsonage garden on St. Agnes is filled with birdsong. Later in the spring, high pressure will bring Mediterranean weather to these lovely islands, and with it a handful of rare visitors. A Hoopoe feeds on the short grass lawn, looking like a black and pink butterfly when it takes to the wing. In the dense pittisporum bushes, a gaudy but shy Golden Oriole delivers its fluty song onto the spring air. Seven hundred miles to the north, on the Shetland island of Fetlar, spring arrives a month or so later. In mid-May, south-easterly winds bring fresh, clear, sunny weather to 'the garden of Shetland'. With the winds comes a fall of spring migrants, drifted across the North Sea en route to their breeding grounds in Scandinavia. Wrynecks and Red-backed Shrikes, once common British breeding birds, but now rare visitors, perch on dry stone walls or on telegraph wires, resting before they resume the last leg of their migratory journey.

Unusual Gardens

AGAINST THE ELEMENTS

Gardeners are resourceful folk, and little details like the prevailing climate won't stop them from trying to create a little patch of green in the most unlikely places. A few miles south of Fetlar, just outside the Shetland capital of Lerwick, lies the hamlet of Asta. Whooper Swans breed on the nearby loch, and Oystercatchers call constantly.

Yet by the road there is a magnificent garden, packed with foliage which shelters one of the most colourful floral displays I have ever seen. Bumblebees float from flower to flower, seemingly oblivious of the biting wind which blows down from the Arctic, even in midsummer. A few years ago, one of the rarest birds ever seen in Britain, a Blue-cheeked Bee-eater, spent a few days in the garden, living up to its name by catching bees, which it ate with great relish before departing, who knows where.

Life on the Isles of Scilly is much easier for the gardener, who can take advantage of exotic plants introduced from the tropics, which thrive in these mild and balmy climes. The Parsonage garden on St. Agnes has long been a favourite amongst twitchers, who peer over the wall in an attempt to catch a glimpse of the latest rare wanderer from North America or Siberia to seek shelter there.

In between these two magnificent examples of the gardener's art are many gardens which don't fit into the neat categories of 'urban', 'suburban' or 'rural'. They include the lighthouse at Portland Bill, or the moat at the bird observatory at Dungeness in Kent. Or perhaps they are hardly 'gardens' at all in the strictest sense, but simply little patches of land by the side of a croft on a remote Hebridean island.

Yet what they have in common is that they attract birds and the more remote the garden, the more unusual the birds are likely to be. True, a Blue Tit may never visit a garden on Shetland, and Jays are very rare visitors to the Isles of Scilly, but the compensation of owning one of these gardens is that whenever you look out

Above: *Pine trees grow well in coastal locations and provide dense, year-round foliage for nesting and roosting birds*

of your window, you never quite know what you will see next!

THINGS TO CONSIDER

If your garden receives the full effect of the prevailing elements, the main things to consider when planning for the birds are how you can provide the maximum amount of shelter for visiting birds, as well as protect the equipment provided for them against the worst effects the weather can bring.

Trees grow slowly, if at all, in many parts of northern Britain, so you may be better off taking advantage of existing features such as dry stone walls. Nevertheless, as visitors to Fair Isle bird observatory know, even the scantiest vegetation by the island's crofts can shelter migrant birds. After crossing the North Sea, they are so exhausted that they are willing to take refuge almost anywhere, provided it gives them temporary respite from the wind and rain.

Wherever you are in the country, the equipment you provide to feed the birds will take a battering from the elements. Make sure bird tables and feeders are as secure as possible, as

---

SUITABLE EQUIPMENT

■ Attempt what you think you will get away with, but bear in mind that the constant battering by the elements will considerably shorten the life of anything made of wood.

■ Try putting up a bird table in the most sheltered part of the garden, making sure that the post is buried as deep as possible to prevent it being blown away!

■ Feeders may be a problem if your garden is windy, though some of the newest models are self-supporting, making it easier for the birds to feed from them.

■ One or two nestboxes, a birdbath and even a pond will help maximise the attraction for the birds.

gale force winds can soon uproot them or blow them away.

PLANTS TO GROW

Your choice of what to grow will be limited by your geographical location. In the northern and western isles, most dwellings have a small patch of land attached to them, where crops are grown. Introducing less typical flowering plants may be a struggle, but as the owner of the garden at Asta has shown, with persistence it can be achieved.

At coastal and island locations farther south you have more options, though you should avoid any plants that might be sensitive to salt spray. In many parts of the south-west, exotic plants will grow freely, and these can often create a more effective shelter against the wind than native varieties.

Apart from these caveats, it's worth experimenting with a variety of plants, and of course checking out what the neighbours are doing; they've probably tried most things over the years, and their advice could save you a lot of time and trouble!

WHAT WILL YOU SEE?

This, more than anything, depends on your location, so I have listed potential species by geography rather than season:

SOUTH-WEST ENGLAND:
■ Spring migrants include swallows, martins, warblers, flycatchers and chats, as well as scarcer ones such as Golden Oriole and Hoopoe. In autumn, you may get even rarer visitors from the east and west, which often seek refuge in gardens after their long and exhausting journey.

NORTH-WEST SCOTLAND:
■ Residents include Hooded Crow and Raven, with House Sparrows and Starlings the commonest small birds. Autumn and winter bring huge invasions of Fieldfare and Redwing from the northwest, together with flocks of finches. Spring and autumn migrants are less obvious than farther south and east, but will include returning Swallows.

THE NORTHERN ISLES:
■ There are very few residents, as many common garden birds are absent from Shetland. Spring and autumn make up for this, however, when almost anything can and does turn up, especially after easterly or south-easterly winds. Wheatears, flycatchers and warblers arrive in large numbers, and in autumn Goldcrests may also be very common. Redwing and Fieldfare also pass through in huge numbers during the autumn.

Above: *Ensure that bird tables are secure and well protected from the elements*

Goldcrest (top right),
Swallow (bottom right),
Willow Warbler (above)

Bird Calendar

Being familiar with the different species of birds likely to be around at different times of the year, and having a good knowledge of their activities in each season, is essential if you are to be successful in creating the perfect environment for the birds in your garden all year round. By making sure that you provide the right amount and type of food to enable birds to survive freezing winter temperatures and summer drought, preparing adequate nesting material in the breeding season or planting the right shrubs or trees, you can make a significant contribution to the quality of life of the birds that visit your garden and make an enormous impact on the numbers and types of birds you will see.

The Bird Calendar that follows takes a month by month look at the kinds of birds you may see in your garden and describes in detail their main activities. For each month there is also a recommended plan of action, with hints on what to do and not do depending on the time of year and the particular requirements of the birds.

THE YEAR AT A GLANCE

WINTER

DECEMBER	PAGES 54–55
JANUARY	PAGES 32–33
FEBRUARY	PAGES 34–35

SPRING

MARCH	PAGES 36–37
APRIL	PAGES 38–39
MAY	PAGES 40–41

SUMMER

JUNE	PAGES 42–43
JULY	PAGES 44–45
AUGUST	PAGES 46–47

AUTUMN

SEPTEMBER	PAGES 48–49
OCTOBER	PAGES 50–51
NOVEMBER	PAGES 52–53

At this time of year, with the weather at its coldest and most severe, the main concern of most of our resident birds is simply how to survive. During this period natural food resources are heavily depleted, and many birds will be forced from the surrounding countryside into gardens as they search for alternative supplies and seek refuge from the harsh winter climate. In addition, cold weather on the Continent may bring influxes of birds such as Fieldfare or Redwing to southern parts of Britain.

Providing a constant supply of quality food for these birds is essential so that they can maintain their energy levels at this particularly testing time of year, but don't forget that water is just as important, as the birds need to keep their plumage in good condition in order to fight the cold.

As the finer spring weather approaches the breeding season begins in earnest. Resident birds start to lay eggs and soon broods of hungry chicks are demanding food from their busy parents. March, April and May also see the arrival of some of our common summer migrants, such as Swallow and House Martin, and by the middle of May, even the latest summer visitors have usually arrived and settled down to breed.

The most important things to remember to do at this time of year are to put out plenty of nesting material for brooding birds, and to ensure that the birds in your garden can continue to benefit from a healthy supply of food, since adult birds can become seriously undernourished as they struggle to provide food for their young.

June, July and August are generally the quietest months for birds in the garden. Early on in the season, young birds may be very much in evidence, often seen in family parties being shown the ropes by their parents. However, as there is a greater availability of natural food supplies at this time of year, they will soon leave with the adults for the wider countryside, not to return until much later in the year. Many birds moult their plumage during the summer months, and as they do so, will hide away from predators, making the bird life yet more difficult to see.

Despite the reduction in activity, you should continue to provide reasonable supplies of food and water, and also pay attention to hygiene and cleanliness as diseases can be a hazard in higher temperatures.

By the time autumn arrives, most summer visitors have departed south for the winter not to return until the following April or May. Natural food may still be plentiful in the surrounding countryside, so the number and range of species of birds you will see will continue to be fairly low, depending on the location of your garden. However, the months of September, October and November also see the first influxes of autumn visitors, including Jays from the Continent, and in northern and eastern parts of the country, the arrival of winter thrushes such as Redwing and Fieldfare from Scandinavia.

Autumn is a good time to carry out basic maintenance such as pruning foliage and cleaning feeding stations and nestboxes, before the really cold weather sets in and in preparation for the main arrival of winter birds.

January

The year often starts with a prolonged spell of harsh winter weather, bringing influxes of birds from the surrounding countryside into rural and suburban gardens. Urban gardens are also full of birds, as the temperature may be several degrees higher than in rural areas, a huge advantage to smaller birds which lose heat rapidly on cold nights. With the short daylight hours, the main concern of most birds is getting enough energy to survive, so feeding activity reaches its peak. But as the days gradually lengthen, the end of the month brings the first snatches of spring song, as species such as Song Thrush and Blackbird prepare to defend their territory and win a mate.

Treecreeper

Song Thrush

ABOVE: *Woodland species such as Treecreeper may be seen seeking refuge in gardens in winter months, while Song Thrushes will become a familiar sight or sound towards the end of January as the days begin to lengthen*

MAIN EVENTS

- Cold spells often force birds to seek refuge in gardens, especially if falls of snow make finding food difficult. Typical visitors include the two winter thrushes, Fieldfare and Redwing, as well as woodland species such as Nuthatch, Treecreeper and Jay. Small birds such as Pied Wagtail also reach their peak.

- If the cold weather is really harsh, you may be visited by water birds such as Grey Heron and Kingfisher, who are unable to find food in their frozen habitat. In really extreme winters, species such as Water Rail and Snipe may even be recorded.

- Look out for unusual garden visitors, especially if you live in the London suburbs, where Ring-necked Parakeets frequently come to feeders in search of their favourite food, peanuts. In southern and western Britain, the mild climate allows Chiffchaffs to overwinter.

- If there is a prolonged spell of harsh winter weather, parts of northern and eastern Britain may seem virtually devoid of birds, which have fled southwards and westwards in search of milder climates and new sources of food.

- Black-headed and Common Gulls reach peak numbers, often dominating the garden with their noisy, squabbling behaviour as they snatch food from each other.

- Later in the month, as the evenings begin to get lighter, watch out for Song Thrushes as they deliver their repetitive but tuneful song from the top of a roof.

January's weather

Traditionally viewed as the coldest month of the year, an honour it in fact shares with February. January can bring very low temperatures indeed – as low as minus 10 degrees C (14 degrees F) or even minus 20 degrees C (minus 4 degrees F) – often accompanied by heavy snowfalls which make it very difficult for birds to find food. The most famous 'Big Freeze' came in 1963, when millions of birds perished, and other freezing Januarys occurred in 1940, 1947 and 1982, when the Scottish town of Braemar experienced the coldest night of the century.

However, January can also be surprisingly mild, with temperatures surging into double figures, especially in southern and western Britain. Early spells of warm and sunny weather can encourage both plants and birds to behave as if spring had already arrived, with disastrous consequences if conditions revert to normal. The recent run of mild winters has reduced winter mortality considerably, allowing small birds such as the Wren to reach near record population levels. January can also be a very stormy month, with the famous 'Burns Day Storm' in 1990 leaving a trail of destruction across the country.

Things to do

The overwhelming concern at this time of year is the birds' continued survival. You can help them in a number of ways:

- Make sure you provide a consistent supply of good quality food. Interrupting the supply or making sudden changes can cause huge problems for your garden birds, which have become dependent on the food you provide.

- Keep your birdbath ice-free, using boiling water to thaw accumulated ice each morning.

- If you haven't already done so, put up new nestboxes or clean existing ones, in good time for the new breeding season.

- January is your last opportunity to carry out basic pruning and tidying, as from February you run the risk of disturbing early nesting birds.

February

As in January, feeding is at the very top of the agenda for garden birds. A typical songbird needs to eat between one-fifth and one-quarter of its body weight every single day, just in order to survive. If it fails to reach that target, it will not have enough body fat to survive the cold nights. At this time of year, with supplies of natural food getting low, it is even more essential that we continue to put out plenty of food for the birds. If the spell of cold weather continues, water for drinking and bathing is almost as important, as birds need to keep their plumage in tip-top condition to fight the cold.

ABOVE: *Flocks of Fieldfares often arrive in southern Britain seeking respite from the harsher winter weather on the Continent*

MAIN EVENTS

- Cold weather on the Continent may force birds to flee westwards to southern Britain. Look out for influxes of Fieldfares and Redwings, or an increase in numbers of Robins and Song Thrushes, especially in southern and eastern Britain.

- Several wintering species reach their peak in gardens, including Long-tailed Tits, Starlings, and various finches such as Chaffinch and Greenfinch. These birds often come into gardens from the surrounding countryside, where supplies of natural food such as weed-seeds have finally run out.

- Chaffinch flocks may also include small numbers of their continental counterpart, Brambling, whose visits to gardens are dependent on the success or failure of their main food supply, beech-mast.

- In urban and suburban gardens, wintering Blackcaps also reach their peak. These birds do not come from the British breeding population, but are visitors from Germany, which have changed their migratory behaviour to spend the winter months in Britain. They thrive here thanks to our generally mild weather and a plentiful supply of food.

- One of the shyest and most unobtrusive garden birds, the Dunnock, boasts an extraordinary sex life. Watch out for pairs of Dunnocks, in which the male jealously shadows the female, guarding her against mating with other, unattached males.

- Courtship behaviour begins to build up to a peak, especially for early breeders such as Collared Dove. Listen out for the drumming of Great Spotted Woodpeckers, and if you live in the country, for the sounds of a nearby rookery. Rooks are one of our earliest breeders, and may have young even before the leaves are on the trees.

FEBRUARY'S WEATHER

February is often the coldest month of the year, with the most prolonged spells of ice and snow. Indeed, February 1947 was the second coldest month this century, with temperatures well below freezing throughout Britain. Such prolonged winter weather wreaks havoc on bird populations, with as many as 90 per cent of birds failing to survive. Despite this, it is rare that harsh winter weather has a long-term effect on bird populations, which have a remarkable ability to recover within a few years.

Conversely, February can also be very mild, as in 1998, when temperatures soared to reach 20 degrees C (68 degrees F) in sheltered parts of south-east England, producing a flurry of spring-like activity. Fortunately, the mild weather continued, and nesters were not penalised for their early start.

THINGS TO DO

As in January, your main concern should be for the birds' survival, especially in prolonged spells of harsh weather.

- Carry on feeding, paying particular attention to the needs of new arrivals, such as Blackcaps and winter thrushes, which thrive on windfall apples. Always make sure your peanut and seed feeders are regularly topped up, and that spilt or uneaten food is cleared away each evening, to avoid unwelcome pests such as rats and mice.

- Take a quick look at your nestboxes, making sure that they are easily accessible to the birds, and that the entrances are not obscured by unnecessary foliage.

- If you have a garden pond, keep it free from ice by using hot water from a kettle or saucepan. However, never use chemicals to melt the water, as this will harm the birds and other pond life.

March

Bird-wise, March is a rather mixed month, with winter visitors building up to a peak before departing north to breed, while the earliest summer migrants begin to arrive in small numbers. Meanwhile, resident breeding species may already be well underway, especially if mild weather allows them to make an early start. Before the month is out, the first eggs will have been laid and, in a few cases, young hatched. Birdsong reaches its peak in March and April, as male birds lay claim to their territories and begin to compete for a mate.

ABOVE: *Chiffchaff is one of the earliest returning summer migrants, usually arriving in rural or suburban gardens near woodland from the middle of the month*

— MAIN EVENTS —

- The breeding season gets truly underway, with resident species such as Blackbird, Robin and Song Thrush all beginning to build nests and lay clutches of eggs.

- As food shortages in the surrounding countryside reach their peak, rural gardens may get visits from large flocks of finches, buntings and sparrows, with scarcer species such as Tree Sparrow, Reed Bunting and Yellowhammer being seen for the first time.

- Other primarily autumn and winter species, such as Goldcrest and Siskin, also reach their peak, again probably as a result of food shortages in their natural habitats. Both species have increased in recent years, due both to their own adaptability and because we provide a greater variety of suitable food.

- Shy, unobtrusive woodland species such as Stock Dove and Lesser Spotted Woodpecker are often at their most visible at this time of year. On warm, sunny days, pairs of Stock Doves may be watched performing their display flight from the tops of tall trees. Meanwhile, Lesser Spotted Woodpeckers may also be seen drumming and calling from the very highest branches, though you may need to look very closely before you see them.

- Our two earliest returning summer migrants, Chiffchaff and Blackcap, may be heard singing their distinctive songs. Chiffchaffs begin to arrive from mid-month, while Blackcaps are usually a week or two later. They are most likely to be heard in suburban or rural gardens near woodland.

- Watch out for birds such as Blue and Great Tits inspecting nestboxes, in preparation for choosing a site to breed.

MARCH'S WEATHER

March, so the old saying goes, 'comes in like a lion and goes out like a lamb'. Would that our weather were so predictable! In fact like any other month, March can show an extraordinary variety of weather, from prolonged freezing spells lasting the whole month, as in the famous winter of 1963, to temperatures peaking above 20 degrees C (68 degrees F), and accompanied by warm, southerly breezes bringing early migrants to our shores, as in 1990.

For birds, the fickleness of March's weather can bring problems: those that breed early may be caught out by a sudden spell of frost and snow late in the month; while those that put off nesting may miss the opportunity to get ahead of their rivals if the weather is good. Meanwhile, migrants can fall foul of stormy weather, which can exact a heavy death toll on exhausted birds.

THINGS TO DO

- As fine spring weather starts to arrive, it can be tempting to reduce the supply of food, or even stop providing it altogether. But remember that with natural food resources at their lowest, and the birds beginning to breed, it is more important than ever that you continue to maintain a healthy food supply.

- If you suspect that a nest is being built in a shrub or bush, resist the temptation to inspect it, as this may put off the parent birds, and cause them to seek out another site. Once the bird is sitting on eggs, however, they will usually tolerate your presence.

- If a nest site seems particularly vulnerable to cats or other predators, try putting up some chicken wire, which allows the parent birds to gain access while putting off predators.

April

'April is the cruellest month…' wrote T. S. Eliot, and although he wasn't thinking about birds, it's certainly true that food shortages at this time of year can cause problems for many species. Modern farming methods including the planting of winter crops mean that the supply of natural food such as weed-seeds has dwindled almost to nothing in many parts of the country. This means that seed-eaters such as finches, buntings and sparrows are especially vulnerable, as there is simply not enough food to go round. April also sees the main arrival of our common summer migrants, including Swallow, House Martin and Willow Warbler, which can be heard singing its delightful song. Meanwhile, our resident birds are reaching the peak of their breeding cycle, with many hungry mouths to feed.

Swallow

Cuckoo

ABOVE: *The Swallow is one of a number of summer visitors which turn up from their African winter-quarters in April. Listen out for the Cuckoo whose call may be heard towards the end of the month*

—— MAIN EVENTS ——

- For most of our resident birds such as tits, finches, thrushes and sparrows, the breeding season is in full swing, with broods of hungry chicks constantly demanding food from their busy parents.

- Common garden breeders such as the House Sparrow reach peak numbers, as they squabble with each other to find the best site to build their untidy nest and raise their noisy young.

- Summer visitors begin to return to this country from their African winter-quarters. These include our two commonest warblers, Willow Warbler and Whitethroat, which can often be heard singing, especially in rural areas. Two other returning migrants, Swallow and House Martin, can be watched hawking for insects during fine spring evenings. By the very end of the month, the first Swifts may have arrived in the extreme south of the country.

- Another summer visitor, the Cuckoo, may also be heard towards the end of the month, though beware of hoaxers or the superficially similar call of the Collared Dove! If fine weather brings light southerly winds, you may even be lucky enough to have a visit from the rare and beautiful Hoopoe, an occasional wanderer from the near Continent.

- In late April, Goldfinches reach their peak numbers in many gardens. These are also returning migrants, which have spent the winter across the Channel. At this time of year there may be very little food for them in the countryside, so garden feeding is vital for their continued survival.

APRIL'S WEATHER

April showers are proverbial, but April can produce the whole range of British weather, from snow and frost, to rain and sun. Cold, wet springs such as that of 1991 delay the arrival of summer migrants, by forcing them to retreat south rather than crossing the Channel in the face of strong northerly winds. If the bad weather continues for the whole month, it can cause widespread breeding failure amongst resident birds, as eggs chill and young starve to death because the parent birds are unable to find enough food.

On the other hand, April can see wonderfully fine weather too, as high pressure over Europe produces light southerly winds, bringing an early heat wave to southern Britain. Meanwhile, at the opposite end of the country in Scotland, late snowfalls are far from uncommon, often delaying the onset of the breeding season by several weeks, and delaying summer visitors such as the Swallow from reaching their final destination.

However, April is usually a fairly dry month in most parts of the country, with the rain, if it comes at all, falling as brief showers.

THINGS TO DO

- Put out nesting material such as hair or wool, which birds can use to line their nests and keep the chicks warm and safe.

- Carry on putting out food, though you may want to switch to 'summer foods' recommended by specialist dealers, such as high-energy sunflower seeds.

- As the temperature rises, don't forget basic hygiene measures such as cleaning out your birdbath regularly to prevent mould forming.

May

May is one of the most active months in the garden, especially if you live in a rural area with a wide selection of breeding birds. By the middle of the month, even the latest summer migrants have usually arrived, and unless the weather is very bad, have settled down to breed. Country gardens aren't the only ones to enjoy a boom in activity; in our towns and cities, the skies are filled with the screaming of Swifts and the twittering of House Martins. Wherever you live, dawn and dusk are marked by a delightful chorus of birdsong, as male birds continue to defend their territories against all-comers. By the end of the month, many young birds have already fledged and left the nest, making constant demands on their parents for food and attention.

ABOVE: *A summer visitor from Africa, the Spotted Flycatcher usually arrives in Britain in May, but has unfortunately fallen in numbers in recent years*

MAIN EVENTS

- The latest summer visitors from Africa, Spotted Flycatcher and Turtle Dove, generally arrive by the middle of the month, and soon begin to advertise their presence by sound and sight. However, in recent years both species have fallen in numbers, and may be absent from many of their former haunts.

- Common migrants such as Swallow and House Martin finally reach the far north, often being the only summer visitors to isolated islands off the north and west of Scotland.

- The main arrival of Swifts usually occurs in the first week of May, although in some years bad weather may delay them by a day or two. Swifts are especially affected by rain, and if May is particularly wet will not begin to breed until the very last week of the month.

- Wood and Feral Pigeons reach their peak in gardens, as the parent birds struggle to gather food for their hungry and demanding young.

- Jackdaws and Jays also reach a peak, with the latter joining Magpies in search of nests where they can grab a quick and easy meal of eggs or young chicks.

MAY'S WEATHER

'Ne'er cast a clout till May is out', goes the old saying, though this probably refers to the plant (may is an old name for Hawthorn) rather than the month. Another saying looks ahead to the harvest season: 'A swarm of bees in May, is worth a load of hay.' Most Mays see a variety of weather conditions, as spells of damp, mild south-westerly winds alternate with brisker, brighter weather from the north and east, bringing frequent and rapid changes. May often sees the greatest contrasts between different parts of the country, with parts of Scotland experiencing long spells of sunny weather while southern Britain suffers from damp, rainy conditions, in a reverse of the traditional pattern.

Although May can bring the first real heat wave conditions, it also often sees the last heavy frosts of the spring. These can suddenly reduce the amount of insect food available for young birds, which need a constant supply of grubs and caterpillars. Wet weather is also a disaster for young birds, as insects may be temporarily unobtainable, so there is a danger they will starve to death.

THINGS TO DO

- If you have House Martins nesting nearby, try putting out some damp mud for them to use to build their nests. One specialist supplier even provides artificial 'mud' for these delightful birds!

- Live food is always welcome, but especially at this time of year, when adult birds can be seriously under-nourished as they strive to provide food for their young.

- If you find a baby bird out of the nest, follow the RSPB Code of Conduct (see Useful Addresses for details). In most circumstances, it is wrong to take the bird into captivity, as its parents are almost certainly able to cope (see pp64–65).

June

Although technically the last of the three spring months, June is very different in character from April and May, and in the bird calendar belongs to summer rather than spring. Most nesting activity is over, though species such as Blackbird and Song Thrush will continue to raise a second, third, fourth or even fifth brood. Young birds are often very much in evidence, spending time in family parties being shown the ropes by their parents before being left alone to fend for themselves. By the end of the month, many birds will have left gardens for the wider countryside, and will not return until much later in the year.

Blue Tit

ABOVE AND RIGHT: *Blue Tits and Great Spotted Woodpeckers can be seen in family parties, with the young learning the tricks of the trade from their parents*

Great Spotted Woodpecker

MAIN EVENTS

- Blackbirds may be on their third or fourth brood, with the female laying a new clutch of eggs while the male continues to feed the young from the previous brood.

- Blue and Great Tits are often seen in family parties, the young birds looking smaller and duller than their parents, and still depending on them to find food.

- Watch out for Great Spotted Woodpeckers coming to feeders, where they have been observed teaching their young how to obtain peanuts!

- The Bullfinch, once common and widespread but now increasingly scarce, may still be seen in some rural gardens. At this time of the year it reaches its peak numbers, as parents continue to feed hungry nestlings.

- If there is a prolonged spell of wet or stormy weather, Swifts will temporarily disappear from their usual haunts. Because they spend their whole lives in the air, they are especially vulnerable to wet weather. When the rains come, the adults flee, while the young enter a state of torpor, reducing their metabolic rate until their parents are able to return up to several days later.

- During fine, sunny weather, you may see Spotted Flycatchers living up to their name, hawking for insects from a low branch or perch on a wall.

- House Martin eggs begin to hatch in early June, and by the end of the month the first chicks will have fledged. Be prepared for a very early morning call as the hungry chicks clamour for food!

JUNE'S WEATHER

'Flaming June' can be taken two ways: as a description or a curse! Like the other spring months, June can be highly variable, both from year to year and in different parts of the country. For example, temperatures have been known to reach more than 35 degrees C (95 degrees F) (during the long hot summer of 1976), while just a year earlier, snow fell during a cricket match in Derbyshire!

June has also given rise to a wealth of weather lore, mostly connected with the coming harvest, such as the saying 'Calm weather in June, sets corn in tune'. But the prize for laconic wit and wisdom must surely go to the anonymous and long-forgotten country sage who observed, one June 24th long ago: 'Before St John's Day, we pray for rain. After that, we get it anyhow.'

THINGS TO DO

- If you own a cat, or have neighbours who do, make sure they are fitted with a bell or other bird-scaring device, to prevent them wreaking havoc amongst the baby birds, which are particularly vulnerable to attack.

- Refill your birdbath more often than normal, especially if the weather is warm, to prevent the water becoming stagnant or running out.

- Continue to provide reasonable supplies of food, though you can reduce the amount for the next few months, as there is more natural food available from this time of year onwards.

July

July is the quietest month in many gardens, as most baby birds have fledged and left with their parents to search for food elsewhere, in surrounding woods or farmland. This is the time of year when most songbirds moult their plumage, shedding their old, worn feathers and replacing them with bright, clean new ones in preparation for the rigours of autumn and winter. Because of this, although they may be present in quite large numbers, most birds are hiding from predators and are therefore very difficult to see. Things have gone quiet sound-wise, too, as male birds no longer have the need to defend a territory or win a mate.

RIGHT: *The Little Owl is a less frequent visitor that may turn up unexpectedly in gardens in midsummer.*

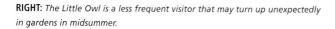

MAIN EVENTS

- Although birds can be hard to see, watch out for family parties of songbirds such as Long-tailed Tits, which advertise their presence by their high-pitched contact calls. They often allow very close approach, seemingly oblivious to your presence.

- Juvenile Robins often appear at this time of year. On first sight they can be quite confusing, as they lack the bright orange-red breast of their parents, and instead have a speckled brown plumage. However, their 'jizz' and behaviour soon gives away their true identity.

- Summer is a good time to observe hunting Sparrowhawks, which feed their young on baby birds.

Sparrowhawks often take advantage of thick foliage to hide, surprising small birds with their sudden attack.

- Warm summer evenings often see large flocks of House Martins and Swifts hawking for insects over urban and suburban skylines. In rural areas, they are joined by Swallows.

- Midsummer is often a time when unusual visitors such as Little Owls turn up unexpectedly in gardens. These may be non-breeding birds, or young birds which have dispersed from their usual breeding areas.

July's Weather

On average, July is the warmest month of the year, with temperatures often reaching 30 degrees C (86 degrees F) or more, although the very hottest days of the year generally occur in August. Prolonged spells of hot weather often lead to drought, which can be a problem for birds with newly-fledged young, which may struggle to find food and water. The successive years of 1975 and 1976 brought the warmest Julys of the century to England and Wales, though these were topped a few years later in July 1983, the warmest month in Britain since records began more than three centuries ago. The period known as the 'dog-days' begins in early July, and is supposed to coincide with a spell of calm, settled weather.

However, July can also be unsettled and cool, especially if the Atlantic weather system dominates. When this happens we get wet and windy conditions from the west, and unless high pressure reasserts itself the weather can be miserable for days or even weeks on end. The best known weather legend of all is linked to July: St. Swithun's Day, in which it is claimed that fair weather or rain on July 15th will continue for forty days. Unfortunately, like much weather folklore, the St. Swithun's Day legend is, in fact, romantic nonsense!

Things to Do

- During hot weather, make sure your birdbath is filled and cleaned regularly, as the water will evaporate rapidly.

- The water level in garden ponds may also drop very quickly. This is unlikely to cause a problem unless the drought is very prolonged, in which case you may wish to top it up occasionally. Avoid chemicals sold to get rid of algae, as they will harm other living creatures in your pond.

- Keep a steady but reduced supply of food, but pay even more attention than usual to hygiene and cleanliness, as disease can be a hazard, especially during warm weather.

August

Like July, August is one of the quietest months for birds in the garden. Natural food resources are widely available elsewhere, and many garden birds spend much of the time in natural habitats such as woodlands and fields. Adult birds are also continuing their moult, so will hide away from predators, often skulking deep inside the foliage of a bush or tree. After a spring and summer filled with the sight and sound of breeding birds, this sudden silence can come as a bit of a shock! Meanwhile, summer visitors prepare to migrate, while resident species are entering the last leg of the breeding season, racing to raise their final brood of young before autumn reduces the supply of available food.

ABOVE: *Keep an eye out for more unusual visitors to your garden, such as the Grey Wagtail*

— MAIN EVENTS —

▨ Some common birds such as Starling and Song Thrush may virtually disappear, as they take their young to nearby areas to take advantage of plentiful supplies of natural food. Nevertheless, some do stay around in gardens, as they know they will get a regular and easily obtainable source of food.

▨ Other birds such as Robins are finishing their summer moult, so may become more visible than during July, especially towards the end of the month.

▨ House Martins and Swallows gather together on telegraph wires in preparation for migration, uttering their delightful twittering calls. They are often joined by juvenile birds, whose tail feathers have not quite grown ready for the long journey ahead.

▨ You may also see the last Swifts, one of the earliest summer visitors to depart on the long journey south to Africa.

▨ As young birds begin to disperse, you may get the odd unusual visitor to the garden, such as Little Owl or Grey Wagtail.

▨ In rural areas, look out for family parties of summer visitors such as Willow Warbler. Although these birds have stopped singing by now, they may be more visible than before as the young birds are less expert at concealing themselves.

AUGUST'S WEATHER

August generally sees the hottest day of the year, with temperatures occasionally reaching 35 degrees C (95 degrees F) in sheltered parts of southern or central England. The four warmest days on record all occurred in August, and include the British record high of 37.1 degrees C (98.8 degrees F), which occurred in Cheltenham, Gloucestershire, on 3rd August 1990. If such hot weather causes a prolonged drought, as in 1976 and 1990, birds continue to suffer from shortages of food and water, so make sure you provide a regular supply.

Nevertheless, August can also bring deluges and floods, either as a result of sudden thunderstorms or unseasonal, heavy rain. Garden birds are less affected by rain than many other species, but if wet conditions are prolonged young birds may suffer from getting wet, or from a lack of suitable food. Generally, however, August weather causes birds few problems, as there is still plenty of natural food available, and temperatures are usually very warm.

THINGS TO DO

- Reduce the food supply to a minimum, but don't stop giving food altogether as birds may go elsewhere permanently, and fail to return later in the year!

- August is a good month to give your feeding station a 'service', scrubbing bird tables and feeders and removing encrusted food.

- Continue to keep your birdbath well-filled and clean, especially during prolonged dry periods.

- Garden ponds may begin to dry out or become clogged with algae, so keep an eye on it if you have one.

- If you own a cat, be especially vigilant at this time of year, as young birds or moulting adults are more vulnerable than usual.

September

Summer is finally over, although natural food supplies remain very high, so gardens continue to have fewer species and lower numbers of birds than the rest of the year. However, September also sees the first influxes of autumn visitors, including Jays from the Continent, and in northern and eastern areas, the first flocks of winter thrushes from Scandinavia, such as Fieldfare and Redwing. By now, young birds have mostly fledged, although there may be a few late broods of Blackbirds still to come. Meanwhile, by the middle of the month most summer visitors have departed south for the winter, and won't be seen again until the following April or May.

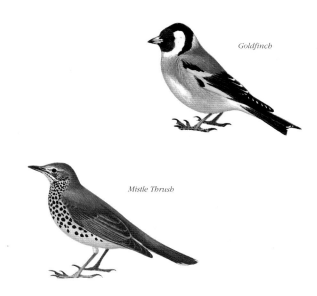

Goldfinch

Mistle Thrush

ABOVE: *Rural gardens may be visited by Goldfinches seeking out supplies of seeds, while Mistle Thrushes prefer to feed on berries*

MAIN EVENTS

- Robins begin to hold autumn territories, and after several months of comparative silence, the sound of birdsong is heard again in gardens as they defend them against intruders.

- Wood Pigeon numbers decline as adults take their young birds to form feeding flocks on nearby farmland. However, Collared Doves generally stay put, especially in suburban areas.

- The first autumn visitors begin to arrive, including in some years influxes of Jays from the north and east. These continental European birds may show subtle plumage variations from their British counterparts, as they belong to a different race or subspecies.

- In northern and eastern parts of the country, flocks of Fieldfares and Redwings begin to arrive, especially following a spell of easterly or north-easterly winds.

They often feed on berry bushes, along with their commoner cousins Song and Mistle Thrushes. This can lead to squabbling between members of the same or different species, as each tries to obtain the most succulent supply of berries.

- House Martins are one of the last common migrants to disappear, and may be very active and noisy as they prepare to depart. Other migrants such as Willow Warbler and Chiffchaff may also pass through gardens on their way south, though they are unlikely to linger for very long.

- Flocks of finches from nearby fields may be seen feeding in rural gardens, taking advantage of plentiful supplies of seeds such as teasels (very popular with Goldfinches, whose beak is specially adapted to obtain the seeds).

SEPTEMBER'S WEATHER

The first official month of autumn, September often sees a great change in the weather, beginning with the remains of an August heat wave and ending with the first gales of autumn. Summer droughts generally come to an end, although temperatures have occasionally reached 35 degrees C (95 degrees F) early on in the month. The end of the month can also bring an 'Indian summer', evocative of Keats' 'season of mists and mellow fruitfulness'.

Westerly gales can cause damage to vegetation, although most gardens are sheltered enough to cope with even the strongest winds. Storms can occur as early as the first week of the month, although the strongest south-westerly winds usually arrive in the final week. Rain-wise, September is on average a drier month than August, especially in eastern parts of the country, although in parts of the south and west the opposite is the case. September also brings the first frosts to many parts of Britain, causing damage to delicate late-flowering plants.

THINGS TO DO

- Keep food supplies at a fairly low level, but don't forget to top up the feeders every day or two, and to provide a reasonable variety of food to attract different species.

- You may want to start to prune shrubs, trees and bushes, though this work may be best left until later in the autumn.

- If you are planning to install a garden pond, this may be the month to do so, as there will be plenty of time for the vegetation to grow before the following summer.

October

Although October can still be a fairly quiet month in the garden, it also sees the main arrival of common winter visitors from continental Europe, such as finches and winter thrushes. Because natural food is still plentiful in many parts of the country, numbers of birds in your garden may be fairly low, although as always this depends on the location of your garden. October is a good month to carry out basic garden maintenance such as pruning foliage and cleaning feeding stations and nestboxes, before the main arrival of winter birds.

ABOVE: *October sees the arrival of flocks of winter visitors like the Redwing*

———— MAIN EVENTS ————

■ Thrushes, finches and sparrows all tend to disappear from gardens, as both adult and young birds exploit plentiful food supplies on nearby farmland or in woodland.

■ At the same time, several species of tit begin to return to gardens, with Coal Tit numbers especially increasing during the month.

■ Listen out for Tawny Owls, which often begin to call to advertise their territory during October. As well as the well-known hooting call, they also utter a piercing 'kee-wick'.

■ Look out for unusual garden visitors such as Chiffchaffs, which are spending the winter here in increasing numbers, especially in the milder parts of south-western Britain.

■ Flocks of winter visitors such as Redwing and Fieldfare may be seen in gardens, especially if you have plenty of berry-bearing shrubs and bushes for them to feed. You may also hear them passing overhead, uttering contact calls as they go.

OCTOBER'S WEATHER

The month of October sees the main transition from the fine, warm conditions of summer and early autumn to the cold weather of late autumn and winter. Temperature-wise, it can range from severe frosts to the mini-heatwave conditions known as an 'Indian summer', which occurred in 1985 and again in 1990. October can also be very wet, holding the record for the wettest month ever in the British Isles, back in 1903. The first heavy snowfalls also often occur during the month, especially in upland parts of northern England and Scotland. October can also be unseasonably cold, as in 1992 and 1993.

The most famous weather event in October – and indeed probably for all time, at least in southern Britain – is the Great Storm of 1987. Despite being considered a disaster at the time, the Great Storm was ultimately very good for birds, as where they weren't cleared away, the fallen trees provided a glut of nest-sites the following spring.

THINGS TO DO

- The nesting season is long over, so October is a good month to clean out nestboxes, removing any debris and nesting material. From October to January you are legally allowed to remove unhatched eggs or dead chicks from nestboxes and dispose of them.

- October is also a good time to prune bushes and shrubs, but make sure you don't cut back the foliage too severely, as this may reveal nesting sites to predators the following spring.

- If you have fruit trees, save windfall apples and pears until later in the winter, when they will provide a very welcome supplementary food for thrushes and Blackbirds at a time when other food resources are scarce.

- Food supplies can be maintained at the same low level as August and September, as natural food is still widely available and there will be fewer birds in your garden.

November

Like March and July, November is a month of transition between the seasons in the bird calendar. Summer visitors are long gone, and most autumn arrivals are well underway, though numbers of wintering birds are long off their peak. Although natural food supplies in the wider countryside are still at fairly high levels, worsening weather may bring an influx of birds into the garden, in search of food. Like October, November is also a good month to carry out basic maintenance tasks before winter sets in, and you lose the enthusiasm to finish them!

ABOVE: *The beautiful Waxwing will occasionally arrive in Britain from Europe in search of its favourite food, berries*

MAIN EVENTS

- Inconspicuous but common birds such as the Wren become far more visible, often foraging in the open for their tiny insect food, or creeping about the base of rockeries, searching inside cracks and crevices.

- The first wintering Blackcaps arrive from central Europe, often visiting bird tables to feed on fruit, or taking advantage of the new supply of berries. This is a relatively recent phenomenon, and the species has clearly been helped by the widespread provision of food in British gardens.

- From time to time, we are treated to an invasion by one of Europe's most beautiful birds, the Waxwing, which sometimes arrive in huge flocks, also in search of berries. They are mainly seen on or near eastern coasts, though they occasionally straggle farther south and west.

- Flocks of Goldcrests may pass through gardens, as they migrate from their northern breeding grounds to milder climes farther south. In southern parts of the country, look out for the rarer Firecrest, distinguished by its brighter plumage and prominent black-and-white head pattern.

- Numbers of Black-headed and Common Gulls begin to build up, especially if there is hard weather farther north. They often visit gardens in large, noisy flocks, terrifying the smaller birds into submission and stealing the choicest morsels of food.

NOVEMBER'S WEATHER

Is there any month as depressing as November? The summer is long gone, and it seems an age until the following spring. No wonder, then, that November's weather lore is hardly filled with optimism, as in the rural rhyme: 'If there's ice in November that will bear a duck, there'll be nothing after but sludge and muck'.

November can be very wet: indeed, of the five wettest months in England and Wales since records began, four have been November – though the most recent was back in 1940. It is also often a very foggy month, as temperatures drop to allow mist and fog to form at dawn or dusk. However, November can also be surprisingly mild and fair at times, with a phenomenon known as 'All Hallows' summer', a brief spell of mild weather supposed to occur at the start of the month. But the last word on this depressing month should go to the poet Thomas Hood, who penned these memorable lines: 'No warmth, no cheerfulness, no healthful ease, No comfortable feel in any member, No shade, no shine, no butterflies, no bees, No fruits, no flowers, no leaves, no birds, No-vember'.

THINGS TO DO

■ Like October, November is a good month to carry out all the annual garden chores such as maintenance and cleaning of feeding stations, bird tables and nestboxes or pruning shrubs and trees.

■ Start to increase the amount and variety of food you put out, as numbers of wintering birds begin to build up.

■ Make sure you keep a regular supply of water for bathing and drinking, paying special attention on cold mornings after frosty nights, when your birdbath may have iced over.

■ If you have a garden pond, make sure that falling leaves haven't clogged it up. Remove them carefully, trying not to disturb the other natural pond vegetation and its inhabitants.

December

The last month of the year may bring the first spell of harsh winter weather to the garden, and along with it the first influx of hungry birds. The quiet period of the autumn is long behind us now, and with luck your efforts during the past year will be beginning to yield results, with an increase in numbers and variety of birds visiting your garden. The Christmas period can provide an opportunity to study your garden's birdlife, observing day-to-day behaviour at really close quarters.

RIGHT: *December usually sees an increase in numbers of the most famous Christmas bird of all, the Robin*

—— MAIN EVENTS ——

■ Berry-eating species such as Mistle Thrush, Fieldfare and Redwing begin to visit gardens in greater numbers than before. Mistle Thrushes often establish a territory on the best berry bushes, fighting off intruders for the rest of the winter, and forcing young birds of their own species to migrate south for the season.

■ The most famous Christmas bird, the Robin, is usually seen in greater numbers. Robins defend territories in winter, and the males can often be heard singing their light, tuneful song from the tops of bushes or trees.

■ If there is a prolonged icy spell, watch out for unusual visitors to your pond, such as Grey Heron or even Kingfisher. These shy birds generally visit early in the morning to avoid being disturbed by humans, but may be observed at close quarters if you are fortunate.

■ During very mild weather, Wood Pigeons and Collared Doves may begin breeding activity, building nests and even laying eggs. This ability to breed throughout the year goes a long way to explaining their success.

■ Watch out for roving flocks of Blue, Great, Coal and Long-tailed Tits, keeping in touch with each other by uttering tiny, high-pitched contact calls. Look closely at each flock, as it may include a more unusual visitor such as a Goldcrest, Treecreeper or even a Lesser Spotted Woodpecker, which tag along with the flock in order to discover the best food supplies.

DECEMBER'S WEATHER

We all know the song 'White Christmas', but in fact snow at this time of year is fairly unusual in most of Britain, as the Christmas period occurs fairly early in the winter season from a chronological point of view. However, December does generally bring the first heavy falls of snow to most parts of northern Britain and the uplands, often forcing birds to seek shelter in gardens as their natural food resources are covered by a blanket of white.

However, even in the worst winters, December is rarely anything like as cold as January or February. Nor is it likely to be particularly wet, though a spell of south-westerlies can bring mild, damp weather more reminiscent of autumn than winter, with temperatures well above freezing.

Weather lore at Christmas is intimately connected with forecasts for the following Easter. Unfortunately, all these long-term forecasts are about as accurate as pure guesswork. But if the weather has been cold and icy in the days leading up to Christmas, take heart from an old English proverb: 'If ice will bear a man before Christmas, it will not bear a mouse afterwards.'

THINGS TO DO

- Make sure you increase the supply of food, especially if there is a spell of cold or wet weather, as the natural food supplies elsewhere are beginning to diminish.

- Do any final maintenance tasks on nest boxes, as birds will begin to prospect likely looking sites early in the New Year, especially if there is a spell of fine weather.

- At Christmas, don't forget the birds! You'll have plenty of spare scraps to put out, including two perennial favourites packed with energy: Christmas cake and Christmas pudding! On a question of taste, turkey is perhaps best avoided.

- Finally, take time to enjoy the fruits of all your hard work during the past year, and the benefit it has brought to the birds in your garden!

Caring for Birds

In order to make your garden as attractive a haven for birds as possible, and to ensure the birds' continued survival, you will need to know the best ways of providing food, shelter, water – for both drinking and bathing – and protection from predators and pests. Each species will have its own particular requirements, depending on, for instance, whether it prefers to eat berries or seeds, whether it is a ground-feeding or arboreal species, or whether it is a hole-nesting species or one which requires a more specialised nestbox, so taking these factors into account when purchasing and setting up the equipment in your garden is also essential.

The section that follows describes in detail how best to care for the birds in your garden, with practical advice on which types of food to use, equipment to install or plants to grow in order to maximise the benefits for the many different types of birds. It tells you how to make the most of the space available in your garden, which particular designs to opt for, how to choose the right site for them and how to get the best use out of your garden's natural features. In addition, there are useful tips on basic garden maintenance, such as hygiene, cleaning and pruning, all of which are important for ensuring the well-being of feeding, nesting and roosting birds.

◀ FEEDING 58–61

This section answers all your questions on the advantages and disadvantages of artificially feeding birds, the best types of food to provide and in what quantities, and the most suitable way of supplying it – be it with a simple peanut feeder, a bird table or a 'space-age'-design feeding station.

▶ NEST SITES AND NESTBOXES 62–65

Learn about different species' nesting habits, the most appropriate design of nestbox to install or trees and shrubs to grow, depending on the birds that visit your garden, and how to choose the right site for them. A special section covers important information on the care of baby birds.

◀ WATER 66–69

With water being as important as food, this section explains why it is vital for birds to be able to drink and bathe regularly, gives practical advice on choosing, installing and maintaining birdbaths, and shows you how to plan a garden pond with useful tips for its upkeep.

▶ PREDATORS AND PESTS 70–73

Whether cats, foxes, rats or other birds, predators and pests need to be controlled. This section looks at the different types of animals that may pose a threat to the birdlife in your garden, and describes the most effective ways of dealing with them.

Feeding

Above: *If you want to attract the widest variety of species, provide different kinds of food at different levels to cater for ground-feeding as well as arboreal species*

Left: *A bird table mounted on a pole in the open should be safe from attacking cats but near enough to a perch for birds to reach it*

When I was growing up in the London suburbs, my grandmother used to save scraps of food and stale bread, which she would fling out on to the lawn for the birds. Later on, at a local pet shop, we bought a small red string bag filled with peanuts, and hung it on the pear tree by the kitchen window. Although it was supposed to attract Greenfinches and even Siskins, the main customers were a flock of House Sparrows!

Until a decade or so ago, this was a typical scene in gardens the length and breadth of Britain. Today, things

are very different. A multi-million pound industry provides thousands of tonnes of food, delivered via a variety of multicoloured feeders and dispensers. If my grandmother were alive today, she might wonder whether all this paraphernalia were really necessary. After all, what was wrong with the old method of throwing out the kitchen leftovers?

In fact, the new approach to bird feeding has a lot to recommend it. A variety of specially designed feeders allows you to attract species with specialised feeding requirements, such

as Goldfinch, which has a marked preference for black sunflower seeds. Putting food on bird tables, rather than the ground, is less likely to attract unwelcome pests such as rats and mice. It is also more hygienic, helping to avoid disease amongst the birds.

Finally, it must be said that most modern feeders are aesthetically pleasing, and help make the process of feeding garden birds a pleasure as well as a duty.

WHY FEED GARDEN BIRDS?

At the end of the day, though, as you're clearing up the discarded food and totting up the bill, you may ask yourself a simple question: does feeding garden birds actually do any good?

The pros and cons of this subject have long been debated, with a few ornithologists fearing that dispensing huge amounts of artificially provided food may cause problems for our birdlife as a whole.

The argument is that artificial feeding can lead to an imbalance between the populations of common birds which readily visit gardens, such as Blue and Great Tits, and their scarcer and shyer relatives, such as Willow Tit, which has suffered a major population decline in recent years.

The debate is a complex one, but mainstream opinion believes that because these species are ecologically separated from one another, an increase in the population of one is unlikely to have any effect on the other.

Meanwhile, consider the positive benefits of feeding birds in your garden. Birds are under constant pressure to replenish lost energy resources, a pressure which becomes acute at two periods of the year: during the breeding season, when hungry chicks have to be fed, and in winter, when ice and snow may make natural food resources temporarily unavailable.

By providing a regular, easily-obtainable supply of food, you are making birds' lives considerably easier, leading to a lower death rate. More birds surviving the winter means more birds to breed the following spring, raising more young – and even more birds to feed the following year!

WHAT YOU NEED TO KNOW

Feeding garden birds may seem simple, but there are a number of things worth considering before you begin:

- Once you've started feeding birds in your garden, don't suddenly stop. The birds will have got used to a regular supply, and may waste valuable energy searching for alternatives.

- Start simply, with a bird table and one or two feeders. Once you have got to know which species regularly visit your garden you can expand your feeding station in order to attract new ones.

- If you want to attract the widest variety of species, provide different kinds of food at different levels, to attract ground-feeding as well as arboreal species.

- Don't forget hygiene: keeping your table and feeders clean and tidy reduces the risk of diseases such as salmonella. Removing surplus food at the end of each day also avoids attracting pests.

- If you can, buy food from approved dealers. It is generally better to avoid peanuts or seed sold in outlets such as pet shops and garden centres, as they may not be suitable.

Above: *A bird table can be fixed to a wall or fence to make the most of the limited space in a small garden*

59

Bird feeders are available in numerous sizes and designs, with multiple 'ports' or squirrel-proof features, to allow greater numbers and types of birds to feed safely

BIRD TABLES

Bird tables have several obvious advantages:

- they allow you to control the area in which the birds feed.

- they attract a wide variety of species.

- you can supply a range of different foods, either placed directly onto the table or from hanging feeders.

- if covered, they provide shelter from rain or snow, and prolong the 'shelf-life' of the food.

- if well-designed they can deter cats from predating on your garden birds.

The basic bird table comes in two designs – with or without a roof – and can be used in three different ways, depending on the design of your garden and the available space:

- mounted on a pole in the ground

- hanging by a chain from a tree

- fixed to a permanent structure such as a wall or garden fence

The ideal site for a bird table is mounted on a pole, in the open enough to deter cats, but near enough to a suitable perch for birds to reach it easily. It should also be easily visible from the back window of your house, so you can observe the birds! It's often worth trying out two or three different locations until you find the ideal one.

All kinds of food are suitable for bird tables: from miscellaneous kitchen scraps to specially-prepared 'bird cakes' made from suet and seeds. Other suitable foods include bread, fruit (dried or fresh), grated cheese, cooked rice, cooked vegetables, and even pet food! However, make sure you avoid very salty foods, as these are harmful to small birds.

OTHER FEEDERS

Specialised bird feeders have come a long way since the red string bag filled with peanuts. Today's feeders are made from tough, durable plastics or metal, and come in a bewildering array of colours and designs, shapes and sizes.

At the basic end of the market, £5 or so will buy you a small peanut or seed feeder, with holes to dispense the food and small perches to allow the birds to reach the contents. If you have plenty of garden visitors, you may need to have several feeders, or buy larger ones, with up to a dozen 'ports'.

Squirrels are a perennial problem in most gardens. The perfect squirrel-proof feeder may not exist, as these ingenious and powerful mammals seem to be able to gain access to most designs. However, a metal cage containing an internal peanut dispenser seems to deter most of these alien pests.

FOOD FOR FEEDERS

The two basic types of food for feeders are peanuts and seeds. The high oil and protein content of peanuts makes them one of the most energy-efficient foods for birds. They are widely available and relatively cheap, although you should avoid the cheapest on the market as they may be contaminated. Thanks to a campaign by the RSPB and bird food manufacturers, the vast majority of peanuts sold are now considered safe for wild birds.

Until relatively recently, the only alternative to peanuts was 'bird seed', a rather dubious mixture of various seeds and grains. Today, however, the wild bird food trade provides an extraordinary variety of seeds designed to attract particular species, such as niger or nyger (a type of sunflower seed) for Goldfinches. In

Above: *A feeder with window pane suckers allows you to view the birds really close*

Right above and below: *Artificially provided niger or nyger seed is ideal for Goldfinches, while fruit-bearing shrubs will offer food for berry-eating species*

addition, the RSPB provides specially-selected mixtures which are suitable for most seed-eating birds.

It is generally best to buy both peanuts and seeds in fairly small quantities, ensuring a rapid turnover. If you do need to store food for longer periods, make sure it is kept in secure bags in a cool, dry place, away from the unwelcome attention of mice or rats. In any case, bird food should normally be used within a few months of purchase.

Many birds, including Robins, Dunnocks, Starlings and Jays, prefer to eat live food such as insects and other invertebrates. A good substitute for natural foods is mealworms, which should be placed in a smooth-sided bowl to prevent escape.

If you have trouble finding bird food locally, there are several mail order companies who will send it directly to your home, saving you the bother of carrying it! (See Useful Addresses for details).

Nest sites and nestboxes

city plot there is room for a couple of dense shrubs in which a pair of Robins can build their nest, or a small area of scrubby bushes suitable for Wrens or Dunnocks.

If your garden is larger, there is plenty of scope for providing opportunities for breeding. Popular garden shrubs such as clematis or barberry are ideal for Blackbirds. Even the much maligned evergreens such as Lawson and Leyland cypresses are perfect nesting places for Greenfinches, which love the dark, dense foliage. Native plants such as elder and hawthorn provide nest sites for a wide range of garden birds, while if you are prepared to be

Providing food for birds will enable them to survive the winter in order to breed the following spring. But as their 'natural' habitat becomes ever scarcer, birds need alternative places to nest and raise their young. If they fail to do so, their population will decline rapidly, perhaps ultimately leading to their extinction as British breeding birds.

This is where we come in. By providing a variety of semi-natural and artificial nest sites, we maximise the chances of successful reproduction. As a by-product, we can enjoy close-up views of breeding behaviour.

There are two main ways in which we can provide nest sites for our garden birds. First, by planting the right variety of bushes, shrubs and trees in which they can safely nest; and second, by providing completely artificial nest sites in the form of nestboxes.

PLANTING FOR NESTING BIRDS

The scope and variety of sites you are able to provide will, of course, depend on the size and location of your garden. But even in the smallest

Above left: *Clematis is ideal for nesting and breeding Blackbirds*

Above: *Native plants like hawthorn provide nest sites for many garden birds*

Right: *A 'tit box' has a small hole in the front to allow entry to hole-nesting species such as Blue and Great Tits*

a little more adventurous, try letting part of your garden 'go wild' by planting bramble bushes.

In the longer term, larger bushes or trees such as yew will eventually provide opportunities for all sorts of birds to nest as well as a healthy supply of berries to feed on afterwards!

NESTBOXES

Modern woodland management abhors untidiness, so dead and dying trees are soon removed and along with them, the opportunities for nesting they provided. Species that rely on natural holes and crevices in which to build their nest, such as tits, are faced with a serious shortage of potential sites.

Again, this is where we can help the birds. In one sense, nestboxes are our small way of compensating the birds for the devastating loss of habitat they have suffered during the past fifty years or so. A good quality, well sited nestbox offers all the advantages of a natural nest site; indeed, it may even prove to be a better place to raise young in the long run.

Nestboxes have one other advantage over natural nest sites. They allow us to enjoy the privilege of watching the intimate details of breeding behaviour from the comfort of our kitchen window, as the birds go about their daily business, unaware that they are putting on a show at the same time.

CHOOSING A NESTBOX

There are almost as many different varieties and designs of nestbox as there are different species of garden birds. Nevertheless, a couple of standard designs cover most of the species likely to nest in your garden, and have the added advantage of

Right: *Robins require an open-fronted nestbox*

being cheap to buy, or if you prefer, easy to make.

When buying a nestbox, it's generally best to avoid elaborate designs such as those often sold as ornaments in garden centres. They may look attractive (although arguably most are hideous!), but when nesting birds are concerned, form and function are far more important than style. So buy your nestbox from a reputable source such as the RSPB or one of the leading bird food suppliers.

NESTBOX DESIGNS

There are two main designs for nestboxes:

1. The 'tit box': a rectangular design with a small hole in the front to allow entry to hole-nesting species such as Blue and Great Tits, House and Tree Sparrows, or Nuthatch, depending on the size of the entrance hole.

2. The open-fronted box: a similar design, but with a large rectangular opening at the front, suitable for species such as Robin, Pied Wagtail and Spotted Flycatcher.

More specialised nestboxes can also be made, including those for specialised nesters such as House Martin or Treecreeper, or larger birds such as Kestrel or Barn Owl.

If you prefer to make rather than buy your nestbox, you can obtain plans for a simple tit box design from the RSPB. If you want to explore more ambitious nestbox designs, the BTO (British Trust of Ornithology) publish an excellent guide: *Nestboxes* by Chris de Feu. (obtainable through the BTO).

SITING A NESTBOX

People often complain that having bought their nestbox and put it up in

their garden, the birds seem to ignore it! While it is certainly true that birds can be very choosy (a pair of Great Tits have finally decided to use a nestbox in my garden after four years!), siting your nestbox in the right place can make a big difference to the chances of it being used.

The basic rules for siting a nestbox are:

- try to have the box in place during the late autumn or early winter, to allow the birds to get used to it.

- fix the box onto something solid, such as a sturdy garden fence, wall or post, between 1.5 and 5 metres (5 and 16 feet) above the ground.

- avoid siting the box where it will receive direct sunlight during the hottest part of the day. In practice, it's best to position the box so that the entrance hole faces any direction between north-east and south-east, or in an area well shaded by foliage.

- try to strike a balance between a site to which the birds can gain easy access, using suitable perches, and one which predators such as cats cannot reach.

Once the box is in place, you need to sit back and be patient, resisting the temptation to inspect the box constantly, as this may disturb the nesting birds and make them desert. If you do wish to inspect the box (for example if you are participating in the BTO's excellent Nest Record Scheme), then follow the BTO's own Code of Conduct (see Further Reading for details).

After the breeding season is over, you may open the box, remove any

nesting material, unhatched eggs or dead young, and give the box a thorough cleaning with boiling water. Whatever you do, avoid strong chemicals, as these may linger and cause harm to the birds the following season. The safest time to clean your nestbox is between October and December.

CARE OF BABY BIRDS

During the period from April to July, when the breeding season is in full swing, the RSPB's Enquiry Unit at its

headquarters at Sandy is deluged with requests for help on one subject. The usual opening line is: 'I've found a baby bird which has fallen out of its nest, and I can't see the parents. What should I do?'

The answer is often: 'do nothing at all'. In most cases, the bird has left the nest of its own accord, and the parents are quite capable of looking after it without our interference. Indeed, by making a fuss over the chick we may be inadvertently preventing the adults from attending to its needs.

In other cases, a chick has fallen from the nest far earlier than it should, and is obviously incapable of surviving in its present state. If you can find the nest, the chick should be put back as soon as possible, though if it has been exposed for more than an hour or so it is unlikely to survive.

Whatever you do, don't try to take the chick into care! If it is unfledged, then it will die anyway; if it is capable of surviving, it has a far better chance out in the wild than with human foster parents.

Above: *Non-standard nestboxes are available for specialised nesters or larger birds such as the Barn Owl*

Ultimately, it is important to remember that the vast majority of young birds die before they reach adulthood: this is nature's way of keeping populations in check. While it may be distressing to see an apparently 'lost' chick calling forlornly for its parents, it is part of the natural cycle of life, and should be regarded as such.

Water: birdbaths and ponds

Above, right and far right: *Providing sufficient amounts of water is a crucial part of caring for birds. A well designed garden will offer ample water features to allow as many different birds as possible to drink and bathe at the same time*

For garden birds, a regular, healthy supply of clean water is almost as important as finding food or a place to nest. That's because water is essential for two aspects of birds' life cycles: drinking and bathing.

WATER FOR DRINKING

Without a regular supply of clean drinking water, birds will dehydrate, especially during hot summer weather. Birds do not drink as frequently as many mammals, as they obtain the majority of water through the moisture in the food they eat. However, most birds drink regularly at least once or twice each day, often in the early morning or late evening. Seed-eaters such as finches and sparrows must drink more frequently than insectivorous species such as warblers, as their food contains a lower proportion of moisture.

When taking a drink, birds are very vulnerable to attack by predators such as cats or Sparrowhawks, so most birds drink quickly and cautiously, often arriving and leaving in small flocks to minimise the chance of being caught.

WATER FOR BATHING

Regular bathing is also vital, as it allows birds to keep their plumage clean and fresh. This is particularly critical if they are to survive cold winter nights, as dirty, matted feathers are far less effective than clean ones against the cold. Only by bathing on a regular basis can birds keep their feathers smooth and clean, allowing the bird to trap air between them as a means of insulation.

Bathing is also intimately linked with preening, during which birds use their beak to separate each feather, removing parasites and generally making sure they are in tip-top condition. You can often watch birds preening after they bathe, sitting in the sun to dry their feathers as they do so.

Many birds bathe at least once a day, often in the morning or evening. Once again, by providing a regular source of clean water, we save the birds the time and trouble of seeking out natural alternatives. During the winter, when they need to feed almost constantly in order to stay alive, this can make a real difference to their chances of survival.

BIRDBATHS

After a bird table, the birdbath is one of the most essential pieces of garden equipment for birds. You can either buy a ready-made bath, or improvise by making your own out of a suitable dish or container. Whatever you do, follow some basic rules:

- avoid fancy ornamental designs sold in garden centres, as they may be unsuitable, especially for smaller birds, which require a well-designed bath.

- make sure your bath is sturdy and solid, with a gentle gradient from shallow to deeper water to allow different sized birds to drink and bathe at the same time.

- make sure the surface of the bath is not too smooth, as birds' feet may slip on it.

- make sure the design enables you to refill the bath with clean water once a day, and also allows you to clean it easily.

- pay particular attention to hygiene, especially during hot, dry weather in summer, when bacteria can build up very rapidly, spreading disease amongst the birds.

- in winter, make sure you keep your birdbath free of ice, by filling it with warm (but not boiling!) water from a kettle or saucepan. During prolonged freezing weather, it is even more essential to provide a regular supply of water for the birds, as their daily survival may depend on it.

Once your birdbath is in position you may be surprised at the variety of species which come to use it. As with bird tables and nestboxes, a well-sited birdbath offers hours of entertainment as you watch the antics and behaviour of your garden birds.

Garden ponds

One of the very best ways to help birds in your garden, and to increase the number and variety of species, is to install a garden pond. In small gardens there may simply not be enough space, but even the smallest pond will improve your garden from the birds' point of view. If you have a large garden, then you can provide something really impressive.

Purple loosestrife (**above**) *and flowering rush* (**right**) *make good plantings at pond margins, and the insect life they attract provides an important food resource for birds*

Garden ponds can help garden birds in several ways. First, by providing a place to drink and bathe, as an alternative to streams, lakes or birdbaths. This is especially useful during periods of hot, dry weather in summer, when alternative sources of water may be scarce, or dry up unexpectedly. Second, by increasing the variety of insect and invertebrate life in your garden, which in turn provides an important food resource for the birds.

From a broader perspective, garden ponds are vital oases for all kinds of other natural creatures, especially frogs and newts, which are becoming more and more scarce as their natural habitat disappears. You'll be amazed at the variety of amphibian and aquatic life your pond can support after just a few months.

PLANNING AND CONSTRUCTING A GARDEN POND

Although making a garden pond may seem a daunting and difficult task, there are various guides on the market which provide step-by-step instructions on how to do so. The key things to remember are:

- Siting: make sure you put the pond in the right place, ideally at the lowest point of your garden (to avoid flooding!), and in an area which receives plenty of sunlight – this is essential for the health of the plant and insect life in your pond. Try to avoid putting the pond directly beneath large trees, as falling leaves will cause problems each autumn.

Left and opposite: *As well as providing an additional source of bathing and drinking water for birds, a garden pond will encourage a great diversity of wildlife*

- Equipment: make sure you have all the right equipment and materials before you start. The best linings are made from thick but flexible butyl rubber, which should be obtainable at most garden centres.

- Planning: pay particular attention to the shape and size of your pond. Mistakes now will be difficult or costly to change later. Take your time to decide how big a pond you want, and the exact shape.

- Planting: it's best to stock your pond with native plants, using a combination of species which provide submerged and floating vegetation, as well as plants which grow around the edge of the pond.

- Another useful tip: 'borrow' a bucketful of water from an established pond, as this will contain all the useful microscopic life you need.

- It's up to you whether or not you decide to stock your pond with exotic fish, though from a purist's point of view it's probably better to stick with native species.

POND MAINTENANCE AND SAFETY

Be prepared to devote time to regular maintenance of your new pond, although once it is well established this shouldn't involve all that much work. Important aspects include:

- removing fallen leaves during the autumn to avoid blocking light into the pond.

- during hot weather or prolonged droughts, clearing algae off the surface of your pond; and occasionally topping up the water level if things get really dry.

- in harsh winter weather, breaking or melting surface ice.

Finally, if you have small children or if young children occasionally visit your garden, make sure that they cannot get access to your pond. Although it is a rare event, each year several children drown in garden ponds. Make sure such a tragedy doesn't happen in yours.

Predators and pests

Above:*The domestic cat is one of the most harmful predators of garden birds*

It can sometimes seem as if you're fighting a losing battle against the army of predators and pests that threaten the birds in your garden. Large or small, conspicuous or elusive, they can wreak havoc with your carefully laid plans. All of them thrive thanks to our direct or indirect encouragement, and getting the better of them takes dedication, ingenuity and a fair amount of good luck!

Predators and pests come in all shapes and sizes, be they cats or squirrels, Sparrowhawks or Magpies, or the unseen rodent visitors that eat spilled food each night after the birds have gone to roost. In addition there is a whole battalion of plant pests, such as aphids, which give many a gardener sleepless nights.

Dealing with these creatures requires the right attitude of mind, in which a certain level of nuisance is considered acceptable, but attempts are made to reduce the worst excesses. No garden is ever going to be completely free from pests and predators, but you can take steps to keep them in check.

CATS

The most harmful killer of all is, ironically, the one we have chosen to introduce into the garden environment: the domestic cat. Despite, or perhaps because of, our affection for these cuddly creatures, we must accept that they are by far the single most important predator of our garden birds.

Figures vary, but it has been reliably estimated that Britain's seven million cats kill anything between thirty and seventy-five million birds every year. This figure may seem incredible, but bear in mind that it only represents each cat making a kill every month or so – hardly an exaggeration of reality.

Worse still, many of our cats have, in recent years, become feral – living without direct help from humans. These cats are very hard to control, as they wander from place to place in search of easy pickings, and because they are not fed directly by us, they are likely to be even more effective killers.

Cats are a major problem for several reasons. The first, and most obvious, is that they are not a natural part of the birds' environment, so like any introduced predator they have a disproportionate effect on populations of natural wildlife. Because we feed and shelter them, they have another unfair advantage over wild birds. Unlike avian predators such as the Magpie and Sparrowhawk, they mainly kill adult birds, which in the longer term is likely to prove more harmful to bird populations.

Proponents of cat welfare argue that their effect on birds has been greatly exaggerated, and that contrary to popular belief they have little or no long term effect on the state of bird populations. Instead, it is argued, cats merely take the surplus birds which would perish anyway because of ill health or injury.

Whichever side of the argument you subscribe to, few would argue against any humane means of reducing the death toll from cat predation. One simple way to do this is to make sure your cat wears a bell, which is supposed to warn birds of its approach. However, some people believe that bells are largely ineffective, and that the only real solution is to use a cat deterrent. These machines emit a high-pitched sound inaudible to the human ear but intolerable to cats, which then make sure they give your garden a wide berth!

MAMMALIAN PREDATORS AND PESTS

Apart from the domestic or feral cat, there are few other mammalian predators of our garden birds. Foxes love taking chickens, but are unlikely to be bothered with most wild birds. Rats take eggs and chicks, as do squirrels, but do not usually harm adult birds.

However, all these animals can be pests, and it is best to avoid encouraging them by keeping food above the ground on bird tables or in feeders (deterring all except the grey squirrel), and by clearing away spilled food every evening, to avoid attracting rats or mice.

The grey squirrel, introduced from North America, presents a much greater problem. Their ability to climb, combined with sharp claws and a very healthy appetite, makes it difficult to deter them. Indeed, a few years ago a BBC television programme took advantage of squirrels' acrobatic habits by setting up complicated obstacle courses in

Right: *Install a specially-designed bird feeder that will deter greedy grey squirrels*

Above: *This peanut cage feeder allows the smaller-sized birds in to feed, while excluding the larger squirrels*

The Magpie **(top)**, *Great Spotted Woodpecker* **(centre)** *and Jay* **(bottom)** *may present a threat by preying on young chicks*

order to find the cleverest and most determined squirrel in the country!

You can buy squirrel-proof feeders, which use a system of closely-spaced metal bars designed to let the small birds in to feed while excluding the larger squirrels. These do work, although they may spoil your enjoyment as you watch the feeding birds.

BIRD PREDATORS

Many birds prey on smaller ones, but in gardens there are three main species of bird predator: the Sparrowhawk, Magpie and Jay.

Magpies and Jays are members of the crow family, and are intelligent, adaptable and opportunistic, always on the lookout for a quick and easy meal. They present the greatest hazard during the breeding season, as they prey mainly on eggs, chicks and newly-fledged young.

Despite newspaper headlines claiming that the Magpie presents the greatest threat to our garden birds, research has shown that the worrying falls in population of many songbirds cannot be blamed on predation, but are largely a result of modern farming methods. Moreover, it is widely believed that the population of any predator (apart from 'unnatural' ones such as the cat) varies in accordance with the availability of its prey – not the other way around. So far from being the villain of the piece, the Magpie (and to a lesser extent the Jay) are simply taking advantage of an easy-to-obtain food supply during the spring and summer months.

The other major predator, the Sparrowhawk, has suffered mixed fortunes over the past few decades. During the 1950s and 1960s, Sparrowhawk populations declined very rapidly, due to the widespread and indiscriminate use of organochlorine pesticides such as DDT. These had the effect of concentrating higher up the food chain, and caused the thinning of eggshells in many birds of prey, including the Sparrowhawk. As a result, the population crashed throughout most of the country.

Since the banning of these harmful pesticides, things have greatly improved. Sparrowhawks are now a familiar sight over most of lowland Britain, and are especially common in leafy, wooded suburbs, towns and even city centres, especially near parks. However, their ability to conceal themselves in foliage, and their habit of flying rapidly from place to place, means that they are not seen as often as you might expect.

Today, it is not an uncommon sight to see a Sparrowhawk flying fast and low into a garden, snatch a feeding bird, and disappear in order to pluck and eat its prey. While this may appear violent, it is important to remember that Blue Tits and other songbirds have been hunted and killed by Sparrowhawks since time immemorial.

Other bird predators include Grey Herons, which can wreak havoc on ornamental fish in your garden pond in a very short time. If you wish, they can be deterred in various ways, including placing a network of wires or string across the surface of your

Above: *Sparrowhawks are birds of prey, and hunt and feed on Blue Tits or other songbirds*

pond, or using a variety of bird scarers which are on the market.

Great Spotted Woodpeckers are another fearsome predator, attacking young chicks by drilling their way into nestboxes to get at the contents. A metal plate fixed over the entrance hole should deter them.

INSECT PESTS

Many gardeners spend much of their time battling against a legion of insect and other invertebrate pests, including aphids, slugs and caterpillars. Much of the damage these creatures do is purely cosmetic, by spoiling the foliage of flowering plants as they feed on it.

You can, of course, use pesticides to control them, but these can be harmful to humans and domestic animals as well as birds, so if you can it is best to avoid them. It is far better to encourage the widest variety of natural predators, such as ladybirds, which eat aphids, Song Thrushes, which feed on slugs and snails, and other small birds such as tits, which feed their young mainly on caterpillars.

Plant Directory

Choosing suitable plants for your garden is obviously a matter of personal choice and preference. Other factors, such as aesthetics and location, also come into play. After all, the birds have to share your garden with its other users! However, there are a number of ways in which you can maximise the benefits for your garden birds, and provide the best possible sources of food, nest sites and shelter, while still keeping your garden looking attractive.

Perhaps the most basic requirement, however large or small your garden, is to provide a good cross section of plants, which in turn provide a variety of plant and animal food for the visiting birds. A bird-friendly garden should have a range of plant types, including:

- seed-bearing plants such as teasel and sunflower, which attract finches, sparrows and buntings, especially during the autumn.
- flowering plants such as honeysuckle and various wild flowers, which attract insects including caterpillars, a vital food resource for young birds during the breeding season.
- berry-bearing plants such as holly, cotoneaster and brambles, which provide high energy food during late summer, autumn and winter for warblers and thrushes.
- if there is room, larger fruiting trees such as apple or oak, which support a huge variety of insect life, as well as providing fruit for a wide range of species including Blackbirds, thrushes and Jays.

All these plants are also good for providing natural nesting sites, and places to shelter or roost in safety from predators during the night. It is also very important to make sure your garden has a variety of plants at different 'levels'; birds such as the Wren and Dunnock nest and feed close to the ground, while other species such as woodpeckers and Nuthatch spend most of their lives in the higher branches or canopy.

NATIVE PLANTS

Where you have a choice, it's generally thought that you should grow native rather than non-native, exotic plants in your garden, especially if you want to attract the widest variety of wildlife. This is not a strict rule, and indeed several non-native plants have proved to be excellent at attracting birds. However, it makes sense, when you consider that each native plant has evolved in conjunction

with a variety of native insects and other invertebrates, so a typical native plant will support a greater variety of grubs, beetles, caterpillars, butterflies and moths than most exotic species.

The very best native plants, if your garden can support them, are large trees such as oak, beech or silver birch. However, growing these from scratch is unlikely to be a practical proposition, so if you're lucky enough to have them, be sure to keep them healthy by having them professionally checked every few years.

Smaller trees such as alder are also excellent for birds, especially in autumn, when the unusually shaped cones provide food for finches, especially roving flocks of Siskin and Redpoll. Willow is also excellent, as it attracts plenty of insect food, especially caterpillars.

The next level down, in terms of size and time to grow, includes fruit trees such as apple or crab apple, and large bushes or hedges such as hawthorn or elder. These take far less time to grow than mature trees, and soon provide a superb resource for the birds, throughout the year. Elder and hawthorn are particularly good for birds, as they provide flowers which attract insects during spring and early summer, berries during late summer and autumn, and cover for nesting and roosting throughout the year. They also look attractive, especially when flowering during the spring.

Climbing plants such as ivy, holly and honeysuckle are also excellent for birds. Ivy and holly are especially useful, as being evergreen they produce fruit later in the season than other berry-bearing plants, often having berries well into the winter, when other sources of food can be very scarce.

Don't forget flowering plants, which are particularly good for attracting butterflies, and of course, provide food for caterpillars. If you can bear them in your garden, stinging nettles are excellent, as are more socially acceptable plants such as nasturtium! Finally, so-called 'weeds' are often excellent seed-providers, attracting flocks of finches during the autumn.

NON-NATIVE PLANTS

Although it is generally preferable to grow native species, don't overlook the possibilities some non-native plants provide. Many are now so widespread and long established as to be virtually indistinguishable from their native counterparts in terms of the insect life they support.

Seed-bearing plants such as honesty and sunflower provide a useful late summer and autumn resource for seed-eating species such as finches and buntings, while the buds of flowering plants such as forsythia are also very popular, especially with Bullfinches.

But it is berry-bearing plants which are the most important amongst the non-native species. Of these, perhaps the best known are pyracantha and cotoneaster, which provide masses of bright red berries, especially popular with winter thrushes such as Fieldfare and Redwing, and with that sought-after invader from Scandinavia, the Waxwing. Flocks of these birds can easily strip a bush bare in just a day or two, before moving on in search of a new supply.

Finally, the much maligned cypresses have been the subject of many a dispute between neighbours, as they grow very rapidly and can easily block out the light in a very short time. However, their dense foliage is very appealing to many garden birds, including Greenfinch, Woodpigeon and Collared Dove, as a safe place to nest and roost. The tiny Goldcrest, a common inhabitant of conifers, will also nest deep inside the dark green foliage.

FALSE ACACIA
Robinia pseudoacacia

Introduced from North America, false acacia is a deciduous, fast-growing tree with an open, domed crown, dark green leaves and, in late spring and early summer, fragrant, pea-like, white flowers borne in dense, drooping clusters. Narrow, flattened, dark brown seed pods ripen in autumn and later open to shed the dark brown seeds.
Height: 25 m (80 ft).

Spread: 15 m (50 ft).
Cultivation: This plant is good for growing in poor, sandy, dry soil. Requires a sunny position and any but waterlogged soil. Protect from strong winds which can damage the brittle branches.
Benefits: Seed-eating birds such as tits, finches and sparrows will be attracted to gardens where false acacia is found growing.

COMMON ALDER
Alnus glutinosa

A medium-sized, deciduous tree, alder is commonly found growing by water especially along the banks of streams and rivers. It bears catkins in late winter or early spring before the glossy, dark green leaves. The male catkins are yellow and drooping; the female catkins, red (see above). Woody, cone-like fruits ripen from green to brown in the autumn and persist long after

the winged seeds have been dispersed.
Height: to 25 m (80 ft).
Spread: 10 m (30 ft).
Cultivation: Grows best in the sun, and thrives in any wet situations, in moist or even waterlogged soil.
Benefits: The seeds in the cones are an attractive source of food to Waxwings, tits, finches, including Goldfinch, Siskin and Redpoll, and Reed Buntings.

CRAB APPLE
Malus 'John Downie'

Malus 'John Downie' is a cultivar of the common crab apple (*Malus sylvestris*), a small, deciduous tree that grows in the wild in hedges, woodland edges and mixed woods. Crab apple cultivars are often grown as lawn ornamentals for their attractive blossoms and edible fruits. Sweet-smelling, white flowers open from pink buds in late spring, and are followed by large, fleshy, red-orange crab apples in autumn.
Height: 10 m (30 ft).
Spread: 7 m (23 ft).
Cultivation: Prefers full sun and will thrive in any fertile, well-drained soil.
Benefits: The autumn crop of apples are enjoyed by Pheasants, Green Woodpeckers, Waxwings, Blackbirds, thrushes and Jays. Fruiting trees support a wide variety of insect life and

other invertebrates, another attraction for birds.

CULTIVATED APPLE
Malus domestica

A deciduous tree with a rounded or domed crown, self-sown specimens are commonly found growing by roads and on waste ground. *Malus domestica* is also popular in gardens where it is widely cultivated for its attractive white or pinkish-white blossom borne in April and May and its edible fruits which usually ripen soft and sweet. There are several cultivars with the shape, size and colour of the fruit varying with each one.
Height: 8–12 m (26–39 ft).
Cultivation: Prefers fairly rich, well-drained soil.
Benefits: Fieldfares, Redwings and Blackbirds may benefit from windfall apples, while insectivorous species will be attracted by an abundance of insects commonly found on this tree. Apple trees are also chosen as nesting sites by Goldfinches.

SILVER BIRCH

Betula pendula

A small, deciduous tree, with slender, drooping branches and silver-white, black-fissured bark, often found on light, dry soils and heaths. Yellow, pendulous (male) and green, erect (female) catkins are produced in early spring, the mature female catkins containing small, winged seeds. The small, bright green leaves are widely spaced, allowing plenty of light through, and turn yellow in autumn.
Height: 20 m (70 ft) and above.
Spread: 10 m (30 ft).
Cultivation: Plant in a sunny position in well-drained soil. Silver birches tolerate exposed sites.
Benefits: Waxwings, Dunnocks, tits, Jays, Magpies, crows, sparrows, finches and Reed Buntings are attracted by the winged seeds, while other species prefer the aphids found on the leaves. The trunks of

mature trees are also ideal for nesting holes. Woodpeckers may choose this tree for a nesting site.

COMMON ELDER

Sambucus nigra

Elder is a deciduous tree or shrub of rather untidy appearance that is common in woodlands or hedgerows, especially in damp places. It often forms colonies and self-sown plants can become dominant in gardens. In June and July it bears strongly scented, creamy-white blossom, followed by large, drooping clusters of berries that ripen from green through to blackish purple in September. The berries contain leathery seeds and birds play an important part in the dispersal of these seeds. Elder retains its leaves until early winter.
Height: to 10 m (30 ft).
Cultivation: Does particularly well in partial shade and rich, moist soil.
Benefits: Waxwings, thrushes, Garden Warblers, crows, starlings and finches are especially drawn to elder by the plentiful berries. Pollinating insects on the summer flowers attract insect-eating species. Elder provides cover for roosting and nesting birds throughout almost the entire year with the Turtle Dove often choosing to build its nest in this tree.

COMMON HAWTHORN

Crataegus monogyna

This deciduous, round-headed tree with spiny twigs is common in hedgerows. A long-lived, slow-growing species, its attractive blossoms and colourful fruits make it valuable for ornamental planting, as well as providing plenty of benefits for birds. From late spring to early summer it produces clusters of fragrant, white flowers, attracting large numbers of insects. The flowers are followed by round, fleshy, green fruits (haws) that ripen to a deep red throughout autumn and early winter.
Height: 10 m (30 ft).
Spread: 8 m (25 ft).
Cultivation: Grows in any soil in sun or part shade. Ideal for gardens in urban, polluted areas as well as in windy, exposed and coastal sites.
Benefits: The fruits provide food for various species of birds, including Pheasants, Waxwings, thrushes, Blue Tits, crows, starlings and finches, while the dense foliage offers a safe place to nest and roost.

BAY LAUREL

Laurus nobilis

An evergreen, broadly conical tree, bay laurel is an introduced species and is usually grown in gardens as a shrub. It also makes an excellent choice in tubs and can be used for topiaries. The dark green, leathery, oval leaves are very aromatic and often used in cooking. The plant produces small, star-shaped, yellow flowers in spring (male and female flowers on separate plants), followed by small, oval berries (on the female tree) that ripen from green to black in autumn.
Height: 12 m (40 ft).
Spread: 10 m (30 ft).
Cultivation: Plant in full sun or partial shade, in well-drained soil and shelter from cold winds. Water freely in dry weather.
Benefits: The berries of bay laurel furnish a valuable supply of high energy food for birds in autumn, while the dense foliage provides cover.

CAPPADOCIAN MAPLE
Acer cappadocium

An introduced species, this maple is a deciduous, spreading tree, popular in gardens for the spectacular autumnal colour it provides. It has one of the best and most reliable golden hues, the five or seven-lobed, bright green leaves turning before those of most other trees in early to mid-October. The yellow flowers are borne after the leaves appear, and are followed by yellowish green, winged fruits with flattened seeds which ripen brown in autumn. The foliage of maples is host to a wide variety of insect pests, a positive benefit being the attraction to birds.
Height: 20 m (70 ft).
Spread: 15 m (50 ft).
Cultivation: Maples require sun or semi-shade and fertile, well-drained soil.
Benefits: The winged fruits and insects on this plant provide a welcome source of food for many species of birds.

COMMON PEAR
Pyrus communis

This small, deciduous, spring-flowering tree is found in the wild in hedgerows and woods. There are several cultivars that are commonly grown in gardens or orchards for their attractive white blossoms, borne in spring before the oval, glossy leaves, and their juicy, edible fruits produced in late summer and autumn.
Height: 15 m (50 ft).
Spread: 10 m (30 ft).
Cultivation: Does best in full sun and requires well-drained soil. Protect from frost and salty coastal winds.
Benefits: The fruits and seeds provide food for Wood Pigeons, Lesser-spotted Woodpeckers, Waxwings, Fieldfares, thrushes, tits, Nuthatches, Jays, Magpies, starlings and finches. Bullfinches will take the buds of this fruit tree in spring. As with all fruit trees, an abundant insect life is associated with the common pear, making it particularly attractive to insectivorous birds.

BLACK PINE
Pinus nigra

This evergreen conifer was introduced to parks and large gardens in Britain in the nineteenth century. It is upright and conical when young, but later becomes wide-spreading with long, heavy branches. It has dense tufts of grey-green, needle-like leaves and bears ovoid to conical, yellow-brown or brown cones that ripen in the second year and contain seeds.
Height: to 40 m (130 ft).
Spread: 1 m (3 ft).
Cultivation: Prefers full sun. Will grow in most types of soil, including dry, sandy, chalk and limestone soils. Pine species are good in coastal locations.
Benefits: Conifers are excellent garden plants as they have year-round foliage, providing good nesting opportunities for birds. Goldcrests especially choose to nest in these trees. Pines are also attractive to seed-eating birds.

LODGEPOLE PINE
Pinus contorta var. *latifolia*

Introduced from the Rocky Mountains, this pine species has been cultivated in Europe in forestry and as an ornamental in gardens. It is a dense, conical or domed conifer with scaly, red-brown bark, slender, twisted, bright green needles and copper-coloured, conical to ovoid cones which mature in the second year.
Height: 15–25 m (50–80 ft).
Cultivation: Prefers full sun and moist soil. Ideal for planting in inhospitable, windy, barren sites, and also tolerates waterlogged soil.
Benefits: Birds are able to nest in the dense, year-round foliage provided by this evergreen tree as well as feed on seeds in cones.

MONTEREY PINE
Pinus radiata

Native to southern California, this is a fast-growing conifer which was introduced here in the nineteenth century. Conical when young, but later becoming domed, the lower, heavy, spreading branches may hang down as far as ground level. The long, slender, needle-like leaves are bright green, contrasting with the grey-black bark, but may turn orange-brown with age or if under stress. The tree produces woody, downward-pointing fruits (cones) that ripen in the autumn or winter of the second year. The cones split open to release seeds though they may be retained unopened on the tree for several years.

Height: to 30 m (100 ft).
Cultivation: Requires full sun and will grow well in rather poor, sandy soils. Tolerant of salt spray, it is good in coastal gardens where it provides an effective wind-break.
Benefits: The dense foliage of this pine tree provides good cover for nesting or roosting birds and the seeds inside the cones are an attractive food source to seed-eating species.

PLUM
Prunus domestica

The cultivated plum is a deciduous tree that bears white flowers in March and April before the short-pointed, blunt-toothed leaves, and sweet, fleshy fruits. It is an attractive choice of tree for gardens, its harvest of plums appealing to the owners and bird visitors alike. There are several subspecies and cultivars (ssp. *damascena* illustrated) and the colour of the fruits varies from purple to red to yellow.

Height: 6–10 m (20–33 ft).
Cultivation: Prefers well-drained soil. Plums flower early so avoid planting them in areas where spring frosts are likely.
Benefits: The fleshy fruits provide a valuable food supply for many species of birds such as Fieldfares, Redwings and Blackbirds. Insect-eating birds will also be attracted by the wide variety of insect life and invertebrates visiting or found living on this tree.

WHITEBEAM
Sorbus aria

A deciduous tree that is commonly found in scrub or woodland edges, is planted in dry, urban streets and cultivated in gardens for its ornamental foliage, flowers and fruits. It is broadly conical when young, but later the crown becomes domed. Branched clusters of heavily fragrant, white flowers appear as the leaves unfurl from May to June, followed by green, spherical or elongated fruits that ripen yellow then scarlet. The leaves turn yellow-brown in autumn.

Height: to 20 m (65 ft).
Cultivation: The leaves, with their felty undersides, are specially designed to prevent water loss so this tree will tolerate dry and exposed locations.
Benefits: The fruits are a useful and highly attractive source of food for several species of birds, including Wood Pigeon, Fieldfares, Redwings, Blackbirds and Mistle Thrushes.

BLACKBERRY, BRAMBLE

Rubus fruticosus

A perennial, deciduous climber that is a common sight in hedgerows, waste places and woods. It is also sometimes cultivated in gardens solely for its juicy, edible fruits which are as popular with humans as with birds. Bramble bears small, white flowers in summer, and fruits that turn from green to red to black as they ripen from August to early October. The prickly leaves turn reddish-purple in autumn.

Height: 3 m (10 ft).
Spread: 3 m (10 ft).
Cultivation: Will grow in any type of soil in sun or shade.
Benefits: If left untrimmed bramble forms an impenetrable thicket, providing plenty of nesting opportunities for birds like Dunnock. Blackberries are an excellent food supply for Wood Pigeons, Waxwings, thrushes, Blackbirds, crows, starlings and finches.

ALPINE CLEMATIS

Clematis alpina

This evergreen, early-flowering clematis is an introduced species and is a particularly hardy and easy-to-manage garden plant. A tall, scrambling climber with attractive foliage, it bears nodding, lantern-shaped, blue flowers singly on long stalks in April or May and long-plumed fruits. The fluffy, silvery seedheads are prominent and remain on the plant until winter.
Height: 2–3 m (6–10 ft).
Spread: 1.5 m (5 ft).

Cultivation: Requires moist, but well-drained soil and sun or partial shade. Well-suited to a north-facing, cool or exposed site. Prune after flowering if required.
Benefits: Seed-eating birds, such as sparrows and finches, will benefit from this plant and Bullfinches, in particular, are known to take the flower buds. The dense tangle of foliage also provides effective cover for birds.

GRAPE VINE

Vitis vinifera

Grape vine, of which there are hundreds of varieties, has been extensively cultivated worldwide principally for the wine-making industry. A deciduous, woody climber with tendrils which it uses to cling to supports, it is ideal for garden trellises or walls where it provides an effective screen with a useful by-product. In May and June it produces green, scented flowers, followed by the rounded, juicy, edible fruits, which may be enjoyed as much by the owners of the

garden as the birds that visit it.
Height: 30 m (100 ft)
Cultivation: Requires well-drained, fertile soil (ideally neutral to alkaline) and full sun or part shade. Protect against late frost.
Benefits: The grapes are a highly attractive food for birds and are eaten by Collared Doves, Ring-necked Parakeets, Green Woodpeckers, Waxwings, thrushes, warblers, tits, crows, starlings and finches.

HONEYSUCKLE   *Lonicera periclymenum*

Honeysuckle is a tall, deciduous, twining climber with woody stems that is well-suited for growing up garden fences or trellises. A native plant, in the wild it is widespread and abundant in hedgerows, woods and scrub. It bears strongly-scented, (becoming noticeably more fragrant in the evening time) white to yellow flowers that are attractive to butterflies from June to October, and shiny, red berries in autumn. The leaves appear in midwinter.
Height: 7 m (23 ft).
Cultivation: Grows in fertile, well-drained soil in sun or semi-shade.
Benefits: Honeysuckle provides plenty of food and cover for birds in a limited space. The fruits are enjoyed by Waxwings, Robins, Blackbirds, Song Thrushes, Garden Warblers, tits, crows and finches. By attracting butterflies, this plant increases the availability of

butterfly larvae, a favourite food of many birds, particularly Cuckoo.

CLIMBING HYDRANGEA   *Hydrangea petiolaris* (syn. *H. anomala* ssp. *petiolaris*)

Hydrangeas are commonly grown in gardens for their showy flowers. This species is a deciduous, woody-stemmed climber that clings to walls or other surfaces with aerial roots and requires plenty of space. Against the attractive, toothed leaves white, lacey flower heads are borne in the summer months. These consist of central female flowers surrounded by a constellation of larger sterile flowers. Climbing hydrangea is perfect for a shady position.
Height and Spread: 7.5 m (25 ft).
Cultivation: Requires sun or semi-shade and moist soil. Prune immediately after flowering if necessary to restrict size.
Benefits: The dense foliage of this wide-spreading climber offers plenty of shelter for garden birds.

HOP   *Humulus lupulus*

A herbaceous, fast-growing, twining climber, this plant is frequently found in the wild in hedgerows, scrub, fens and wet woods, but is ideal for an arch or pergola in a garden and for concealing unsightly sheds or tree stumps. It has toothed, deeply-lobed, greenish-yellow leaves and from July to September bears greenish flowers. The male flowers are produced in branched clusters while the spikes of female flowers, which are borne on separate plants, become drooping, cone-like clusters of 'hops' in autumn and have a distinct, heavy odour.
Height: to 6 m (20 ft).
Cultivation: Requires sun and moist, fertile soil.
Benefits: Like other climbers, fast-growing hop provides a good cover of foliage for birds to shelter in.

IVY
Hedera helix

A widespread and abundant plant found in the wild in woods, hedges and on rocks. This woody-stemmed climber grows thickly up tree trunks, walls and fences by means of clinging tendrils, or spreads rapidly over ground. The leaves are evergreen, glossy and lobed. Small clusters of yellowish-green flowers that attract a variety of pollinating insects are produced in autumn, whilst berries ripen from January through to spring providing high energy food for birds during winter months when other food sources are scarce.
Height: 10 m (30 ft).
Spread: 5 m (15 ft).
Cultivation: Prefers well-drained soils. Tolerates shade but will only flower in the sun.
Benefits: Berries are a valuable food source for birds in winter. Wood Pigeons, Collared Doves, Waxwings, thrushes, Jays, Starlings and finches all feed on them. Ivy also provides dense cover for nesting Wrens and other species. If flowering, ivy attracts insects, an added attraction for the birds in your garden.

VIRGINIA CREEPER
Parthenocissus quinquefolia

A fast-growing, deciduous, tendril climber with woody stems, ideal for high walls or buildings. It is often grown in gardens for its ornamental leaves which turn a beautiful crimson or purple colour in autumn. At the same time it produces blue-black berries that are a favourite of birds.
Height: 15 m (50 ft) or more.
Cultivation: Grow in fertile, well-drained soil, in sun or semi-shade. Prune back in winter.
Benefits: The berries may be enjoyed by various species of birds, including Mistle Thrushes, Magpies, crows and Redpolls. This plant also provides cover for birds.

WISTERIA
Wisteria sinensis

Wisteria is a deciduous, woody-stemmed, twining climber that is commonly grown up the walls of buildings. A non-native plant, it bears fragrant, lilac flowers in racemes 20–30 cm (8–12 in) long in early summer, followed by velvety seed pods.
Height: to 30 m (100 ft).
Cultivation: Will grow in almost any soil, but thrives best in a deep, rich soil that does not become too dry. Requires sun or partial shade.
Benefits: As well as being attractive in its own right, this climbing plant is excellent for providing cover for various species of nesting birds. The scented flowers attract insects during the summer months, increasing the opportunities for insect-eating birds, especially flycatchers and warblers, to find food.

BARBERRY
Berberis thunbergii

Barberry species are usually cultivated for their attractive flowers and foliage and colourful fruits. With its thick, prickly growth it also makes a particularly effective intruder-proof hedge. *Berberis thunbergii* is a deciduous, dense shrub with oval, pale to mid-green leaves that take on brilliant hues in autumn. In spring small, pale yellow flowers appear, followed by egg-shaped, bright red fruits.
Height: 2 m (6 ft).
Spread: 3 m (10ft).
Cultivation: Requires sun or semi-shade and well-drained soil.
Benefits: The bright red, juicy berries that follow the flowers are ideal for winter thrushes such as Fieldfare, Redwing or Waxwing. Roosting and nesting birds can also take advantage of the cover offered by this dense bush.

A BROOM
Genista lydia

This deciduous, domed shrub has slender, arching branches and tiny, blue-green leaves. Pea-like, bright yellow flowers are borne in terminal clusters in late spring and early summer. Flat seed pods form later in the season, after flowering. This plant is ideal for trailing over rocks in rock gardens, or a wall.
Height: 45–60 cm (1.5–2 ft).
Spread: 60 cm (2 ft) or more.
Cultivation: Will grow in poor, dry soil and does best in full sun. Good for hot, dry situations.
Benefits: Insects attracted to the colourful flowers and seed pods provide food for birds. In addition, birds may seek cover in the dense branches of this shrub.

BUTTERFLY BUSH
Buddleia davidii

This is a vigorous, deciduous shrub which produces fragrant, violet-purple flowers in long, arching spikes from midsummer to autumn. Leaves are long, lance-shaped and dark green with felty undersides. As its common name suggests, the flowers of this plant are highly attractive to butterflies.
Height and Spread: 5 m (15 ft).
Cultivation: Requires full sun and fertile, well-drained soil.

Can become very unruly so cut back hard in spring.
Benefits: The insect life associated with this plant makes it attractive to a number of insect-eating birds. In particular, the large number of butterflies visiting this plant increases the chances for good populations of butterfly larvae and caterpillars, an important food for many species including Cuckoos and tits.

RED-BERRIED ELDER *Sambucus racemosa*

Sambucus species are usually grown for their attractive foliage, flowers and fruits. An introduced species, red-berried

elder is a deciduous, bushy shrub. The mid-green leaves consist of five oval leaflets and in spring the plant produces creamy-yellow flowers, which are smaller than those of common elder, are borne in dense, conical clusters and attract large numbers of insects. The flowers are followed by spherical, red fruits that are particularly attractive to birds. Red-berried elder makes a smaller shrub than elder.
Height and Spread: 3 m (10 ft).
Cultivation: Requires fertile, moist soil, and sun.
Benefits: Berry-eating birds, such as Waxwings and thrushes, will be attracted by the valuable supply of fruits provided by this plant, while insects drawn to the flowers in spring encourage insectivorous species. Being a dense shrub, red-berried elder also provides good cover for birds.

GOOSEBERRY *Ribes uva-crispa*

Gooseberry grows in the wild in woods, scrub and hedgerows but is also widely cultivated for its edible fruits. A branching, spiny shrub it produces small, green, purple-tinged flowers in spring, followed by sour, hairy, green fruits (gooseberries) from May to August. It can be grown as a bush or trained against a wall.
Height: 1.5 m (5 ft).
Spread: 75 cm (2.5 ft).
Cultivation: Requires full sun and fertile, well-drained soil. Keep roots moist and prune bush to improve fruiting and prevent mildew.
Benefits: Blackbirds in particular favour the fruits of this plant while other species may seek shelter in its dense, spiny growth.

GORSE *Ulex europaeus*

This is an evergreen, bushy shrub with spiny leaves and shoots and is a familiar sight on heaths and grassland. In gardens it is commonly grown for its fragrant, sunny, golden-yellow flowers, which are borne on stalked spikes almost all year long and attract a wide variety of pollinating insects, including flies, beetles and butterflies.

Height: 1 m (3 ft).
Spread: 1.5 m (5 ft).
Cultivation: Prefers full sun and poor, well-drained, acid soil.
Benefits: This plant supports a wide range of insects, making it particularly attractive to insect-eating birds. With its spines offering protection from predators, it also makes a good nesting site.

TWISTED HAZEL *Corylus avellana 'Contorta'*

Hazel (*Corylus avellana*) is a native plant commonly found in the wild in wood scrub and hedges. A few cultivars have been developed for gardens, including the fairly common twisted hazel. This is a deciduous, bushy shrub which, as its name suggests, has rather attractive twisted, curled shoots and broad, sharply-toothed, mid-green leaves. The flowers appear long before the leaves, the bare branches becoming covered with drooping, pale yellow catkins (male flowers) in late winter. The edible fruits are in the form of clusters of two to four brown, smooth, woody-shelled nuts covered by leafy growth.
Height and Spread: 5 m (16.5 ft).
Cultivation: Prefers full sun or partial shade and well-drained soil.
Benefits: The fruits provide nutritious food for various species of birds.

LADY'S EARDROPS   *Fuchsia magellanica*

Introduced from Chile, this fuchsia, commonly known as Lady's Eardrops on account of the shape of the flowers, is one of the hardiest and most manageable species. It forms a deciduous, upright shrub that is popular in gardens for its reliable and long season of flowering. The small, colourful, rather delicate-looking flowers have red tubes, long, red sepals, and purple petals, and are usually borne from early summer to autumn in hanging clusters. They are followed by black fruits. There are several cultivars and varieties.

Height: 3 m (10 ft).
Spread: 2 m (6 ft).
Cultivation: This plant requires a sheltered, partially shaded position and fertile, moist but well-drained soil. Fuchsias will grow larger in milder areas.
Benefits: Birds can benefit from the cover provided by this shrub, while the fruits may be a useful source of food at times when other resources are stretched.

LAVENDER   *Lavandula angustifolia*

Often grown as an ornamental plant, this evergreen, bushy shrub has silvery-green, aromatic leaves and bears spikes of purple, fragrant flowers from mid to late summer, followed by small fruits. A number of varieties exist, for example 'Hidcote Pink' (illustrated), which has pinkinsh flowers. Lavender is good for encouraging the wildlife in your garden by attracting bees, butterflies and other flying insects. Ideal for the wild flower garden, it also makes an effective low hedge.

Height: 30–60 cm (1–2 ft).
Spread: 30–60 cm (1–2 ft).
Cultivation: Prefers full sun and fertile, well-drained soil. Clip lightly after flowering and in spring.
Benefits: Goldfinches feed on the dry seedheads and insect-eating species, such as flycatchers, Swallows and House Martins will be encouraged by the large number of flying insects drawn to this plant. Lavender also provides good nesting material.

LAURUSTINUS   *Viburnum tinus*

Laurustinus is widely grown in gardens for its foliage, flowers and fruits. It is an evergreen, dense, bushy shrub with oval, glossy, dark green leaves and clusters of white flowers which open from pink buds during late winter and spring. The flowers are followed by black fruits. This plant makes a good sheared hedge.

Height: 3 m (10 ft).
Spread: 3 m (10 ft).
Cultivation: Prefers sun or partial shade and moist but well-drained soil. Grow where it is sheltered from wind.
Benefits: The fruits may be taken by various species of birds and the dense foliage offers a safe place for birds to seek shelter.

LAVENDER COTTON   *Santolina chamaecyparissus*

The shoots of this evergreen, rounded, dense shrub are covered with woolly, white growth as are the aromatic, narrow, finely-toothed leaves, creating a rather attractive sea of silver in the garden. In mid and late summer the plant carries button-like heads of small, pale yellow flowers borne on long stems.

Height: 75 cm (2.5 ft).
Spread: 1 m (3 ft).
Cultivation: Requires sun and not too rich, well-drained soil. To maintain neatness trim back each year after the flowers fade. This makes a good coastal garden plant.
Benefits: Insects are attracted to the colourful flowers, which in turn encourages the birdlife in your garden. Birds may also use the cover provided by this dense shrub.

OLEARIA x HAASTII

The daisy bushes (*Olearia*), are evergreen, dense shrubs commonly grown for their foliage and scented flowers. Ideal for creating a hedge, in mild, coastal areas they also serve as a highly effective windbreak. This species has small, grey-green, glossy leaves with silvery-white undersides, and from mid to late summer becomes covered with fragrant, daisy-like, white flowers. The flowers are followed by many seeds with hairy parasols.
Height and Spread: to 2 m (6 ft).
Cultivation: Will grow in full sun or partial shade and well-drained soil. Will also tolerate coastal conditions.
Benefits: Seed-eating birds may be attracted to this plant as well as birds looking for cover.

The fragrant flowers will attract insects in the summer months, another attraction for the birdlife.

PYRACANTHA 'ORANGE GLOW'

A popular garden ornamental, usually grown for its attractive foliage, flowers and fruit, this evergreen shrub has oblong, dark green leaves and clusters of small, five-petalled, white flowers borne in early summer. The flowers are followed by many spherical, brilliant orange fruits. *Pyracantha* species are particularly versatile garden plants, useful for creating a hedge, as dense bushes in the shrub border or even for covering a slope.
Height: 5 m (15 ft).
Spread: 3 m (10 ft).
Cultivation: Grow in a sheltered site in sun or semi-shade and fertile soil.
Benefits: The berries are highly inviting for birds especially Wood Pigeons and winter thrushes. This dense, spiny shrub also provides a safe nesting place.

PERIWINKLE   *Vinca* spp.

Periwinkles are found growing in the wild on rocks and in woods and hedge-banks but these evergreen, prostrate shrubs with dark green, glossy leaves and tubular flowers are frequently grown in the garden where they are useful for ground cover. Greater periwinkle is more arching and produces large, bright blue flowers from late spring to early autumn, while lesser periwinkle (illustrated) is a spreading, mat-forming shrub, and bears purple, blue or white flowers mainly from mid-spring to early summer, followed by elongated, forked fruits.
Height : 45 cm (1.5 ft) (greater periwinkle).
Spread: 1.5 m (5 ft) or more.
Cultivation: Grow in part shade and moist but well-drained soil. Will flower more freely given some sun.
Benefits: These low-growing shrubs provide cover and may harbour good populations of insects and spiders, an attractive food source for many birds, especially the more shy, ground-feeding species such as Dunnock.

DOG ROSE   *Rosa canina*

This deciduous, climbing shrub is a common sight in woods and hedgerows. The pretty, pink or white flowers open in summer and are followed by red, seed-laden fruits (hips), which ripen in September and remain juicy until the end of winter when they turn black and shrivel.
Height: 3 m.
Cultivation: Requires fertile soil and sun. Trim in winter and prune in February to allow fruiting.
Benefits: Wood Pigeons, Waxwings, thrushes, Garden Warblers, tits, Jays, Magpies and finches feed on the fruits. Aphids on leaves attract other birds, such as Blue Tits or House Sparrows. The thick growth also offers a useful nesting site for Song Thrushes or Blackbirds.

GUELDER ROSE

Viburnum opulus

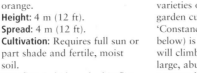

A deciduous, bushy shrub or small tree that is found growing in the wild in damp woods, fens, scrub and hedges. Its foliage, which takes on beautiful hues in the autumn, and the appealing bright red fruits make it a popular choice in gardens. It has broad, lobed, ivy-like leaves and, in late spring and early summer, bears clusters of showy, white flowers followed by large bunches of spherical, juicy, red berries in autumn. At the same time the deep green leaves turn autumnal shades of red and orange.

Height: 4 m (12 ft).
Spread: 4 m (12 ft).
Cultivation: Requires full sun or part shade and fertile, moist soil.
Benefits: Aphids and whiteflies, which some bird species feed on, are common on the foliage of this plant. The berries are also an attractive food source for Collared Doves, Waxwings, thrushes, Garden Warblers and Jays.

SHRUB ROSES

There are numerous species and varieties of shrub roses for garden cultivation. *Rosa* 'Constance Spry' (illustrated below) is an arching rose that will climb if supported. It has large, abundant leaves and in summer bears cupped, pink, scented flowers.

Height: 2 m (6 ft).
Spread: 1.5 m (5 ft).
Rosa moyesii is another arching, vigorous species. In addition to the dusky-scarlet flowers that appear in summer, it carries long red fruits (hips) in autumn (illustratedopposite). Leaves are small, dark green and sparse.

Height: 4 m (12 ft).
Spread: 3 m (10 ft).
The somewhat unruly, but attractive hedgehog rose (*Rosa rugosa*) also produces large red hips. Its fragrant flowers are white or purple-red and appear in summer and autumn.

Height: 1–2 m (3–6 ft).
Spread: 1–2 m (3–6 ft).
Cultivation: All prefer full sun and well-drained soil.
Benefits: The fruits (hips) of roses are enjoyed by various species of birds. Roses are host to a large number of insects, especially aphids, which provides another benefit for the birdlife.

ROSEMARY

Rosmarinus officinalis

Rosemary is an evergreen, dense shrub that has been cultivated for centuries, mainly for its aromatic, needle-like leaves, which are used as a culinary herb or for extracting oil for use in medicine. In gardens it makes a very good ornamental plant, doing particularly well as an informal hedge. Small, purple-blue flowers are borne in loose clusters from mid-spring to early summer and are highly attractive to bees. This plant may also be grown in a pot.

Height: 1.5 m (5 ft).
Spread: 1.5 m (5 ft).
Cultivation: Prefers full sun and well-drained soil. Shelter from cold winds.
Benefits: Insect-eating birds, such as Spotted Flycatchers, which feed on bees and other flying insects, will benefit from the presence of this plant. Good for providing cover for birds also.

PURPLE SAGE   *Salvia officinalis 'Purpurascens'*

Sage is often grown in gardens for its tubular, brightly coloured flowers and aromatic foliage which can be dried for use as a culinary herb. This purple-variegated form is an evergreen or semi-evergreen, bushy shrub, the oblong, grey-green leaves of which are flushed purple when young. In summer it bears blue-purple flowers. This plant does equally well as a pot plant, planted in the herb garden or in the flower border.
Height: 60 cm (2 ft).
Spread: 1 m (3 ft).
Cultivation: Requires full sun and fertile, well-drained soil. Shelter from cold winds.
Benefits: This bushy shrub provides effective cover for birds.

ST JOHN'S WORT   *Hypericum perforatum*

St John's wort is an evergreen, perennial shrub commonly found in grassy places and open woods. It spreads rapidly to form a dense carpet and therefore makes an ideal plant for rock gardens or borders. The yellow, star-shaped flowers are produced from June to September and attract pollinating insects such as bees and flies.
Height: 90 cm (3 ft).
Spread: Indefinite.
Cultivation: Requires moist soil in sun or part-shade.
Benefits: Pollinating insects on or near the flowers are an attraction of this plant to some species of birds while the seeds are eaten by Redpolls and Bullfinches. This carpet-forming plant also provides cover for birds foraging on the ground.

WALL-SPRAY   *Cotoneaster horizontalis*

Cotoneasters are popular ornamental plants, often chosen for their attractive habit of growth, their rich fruits and their foliage, which in some species takes on a brilliant colouring in the autumn. This is a deciduous, rigid-branched, spreading shrub with compact foliage, and is ideal for walls, banks or ground cover. From late spring to early summer pinkish-white flowers are produced, followed by a profusion of red fruits which last until midwinter. The neat, dark green leaves turn a brilliant red in late autumn.
Height: 60 cm (2 ft).
Spread: 1.5 m (5 ft).
Cultivation: Prefers sun and well-drained soil. Will tolerate a dry situation.
Benefits: The compact foliage provides good cover for birds. Winter thrushes such as Fieldfare, Redwing or Waxwing feed on the juicy, nutritious berries.

AMARANTH

Amaranthus spp.

Usually found growing in waste places, common amaranth (*Amaranthus retroflexus*) is a hairy, much-branched perennial that bears tiny flowers on densely crowded spikes, while white amaranth (*A. albus*, illustrated) is hairless, with whitish stems and greenish flowers with bristle-like bracts. These plants are ideal for wild flower gardens, attracting a variety of insect life and therefore encouraging the birdlife.
Height: 30–60 cm (1–2 ft) or more.
Cultivation: Grow in a sunny position in well-drained soil.
Benefits: The seeds of these 'weed' plants are highly attractive to seed-eating birds. Birds may also be attracted by an abundance of insects commonly found on these plants.

WILD ANGELICA

Angelica sylvestris

This tall perennial is often found in damp situations, and is well-suited to growing by a garden pond or stream. It is sometimes used as a culinary herb. White or pink flowers are produced from July to September in the third year, followed by winged fruits. The flowers attract a large number of pollinating insects, while pests such as slugs, snails and aphids are commonly found on the foliage.
Height: 2 m (6.5 ft).
Spread: 1 m (3 ft).
Cultivation: Grow in deep, moist, fertile loam soil, ideally in full sun. Best grown as a biennial.
Benefits: Slugs and snails found on the leaves are an especially important food for Song Thrushes, while seeds are eaten by Blue Tits and Greenfinches. Pollinating insects in summer attract other insect-eating birds.

ARUM PICTUM

This is an autumn-flowering tuber of rather striking appearance. Arrow-shaped, semi-erect, glossy leaves with cream veins are produced at the same time as a deep purple-brown sheath (spathe) and dark purple spike (spadix).

Height: 15–25 cm (6–10 in).
Spread: 15–20 cm (6–8 in).
Cultivation: Requires full sun and moist soil.
Benefits: The berries produced by this plant are a highly attractive source of food for birds.

RUNNER BEAN

Phaseolus coccineus

Usually grown as an annual, this tall, slender twiner produces bright scarlet flowers making it a good ornamental on porches and arbours as well as a productive vegetable. The long, edible pods contain three or four large seeds that ripen to a brown, red or black colour.
Height: to 2.5 m (8 ft).
Cultivation: Fertile soils where the roots are always cool and moist will ensure a good crop. Dig and manure the ground thoroughly before sowing seeds or planting out young plants. Seeds should be sown 5 cm (2 in) deep and 15–20 cm (6–8 in) apart. Provide support, especially for the top heavy growth, in the form of canes.
Benefits: Some birds are attracted to the flowers of runner beans.

BISTORT
Persicaria bistorta

A vigorous, clump-forming perennial, bistort is a weed and is often found growing in meadows or on verges. Ideal for 'wild' gardens, it produces dense spikes of pink flowers from early to late summer, followed by brownish-red fruits in the autumn.
Height: 60–75 cm (2–2.5 ft).
Spread: 60 cm (2 ft).

Cultivation: Prefers any moist but well-drained soil, in sun or part shade.
Benefits: Many birds, including Collared Doves, Pheasants, Black-headed Gulls, Dunnocks, finches, crows and sparrows, will eat the seeds. The flowers also attract pollinating insects, providing food for insectivorous species.

MEADOW BUTTERCUP
Ranunculus acris

Commonly found in the wild in meadows and damp, grassy places, this is a hairy perennial with shiny, golden-yellow flowers borne from April to October. It can be grown in the flower garden or rockery.

Height: 30–60 cm (1–2 ft).
Cultivation: Grows in sun or partial shade, in moist but well-drained soil.
Benefits: This plant attracts a wide variety of insects including flies and beetles.

CARDOON
Cynara cardunculus

This ornamental plant is closely related to the globe artichoke, *Cynara scolymus*. A perennial, it has large clumps of arching, deeply-jagged, silver-grey leaves and distinctive, thistle-like, blue-purple flower heads borne on stout, grey stems throughout summer. The flowers are

attractive to bees.
Height: 2 m (6 ft).
Spread: 1 m (3 ft).
Cultivation: Prefers sun and well-drained soil.
Benefits: Flycatchers eat bees, which are drawn to this plant in large numbers.

COMMON COMFREY
Symphytum officinale

This medium to tall perennial is commonly found growing in damp habitats such as river and stream margins, woodland, fens and ditches. It is an ideal plant for a 'wild garden' where it forms bushy clumps and grows well under trees or in shady borders. The plant has been used throughout history for its medicinal and healing properties and as a herbal. It has large, coarse leaves and from May to July bears violet-purple, pink or white, tubular flowers in branched, nodding clusters. The flowers attract pollinating insects, especially bees.
Height: 60–120 cm (2–4ft).
Cultivation: Prefers damp soil (not acid) and part shade.
Benefits: Insects attracted to the colourful flowers are an attraction for many species of birds.

CORN COCKLE

Agrostemma githago

Mainly found in the wild on arable land such as cornfields, corn cockle is a fast-growing, erect annual with lance-shaped, grey-green leaves. In summer it produces open, trumpet-shaped, pink flowers borne on slender, downy stems. Seeds are tiny, dark brown and poisonous.
Height: 60 cm–1 m (2–3 ft).
Spread: 30 cm (1 ft).
Cultivation: Prefers full sun and well-drained soil. Support with sticks and dead-head to prolong flowering.
Benefits: In summer the flowers attract pollinating insects such as butterflies, an important attraction for the birdlife in your garden.

CORNFLOWER

Centaurea cyanus

A fast-growing, upright annual. It has grey-green leaves, and in summer and early autumn, the branching stems bear double, daisy-like flower heads in shades of blue, pink, purple, red or white. Cornflowers are ideal for naturalising in grass, and attract bees and butterflies. They may also be grown in a pot for winter flowering.

Height: 1 m (3 ft).
Spread: 30 cm (1 ft).
Cultivation: Requires sun and well-drained soil.
Benefits: A variety of insects visit the flowers in summer making it attractive to insect-eating birds. The seeds are eaten by Blue Tits, Carrion Crows, Greenfinches and Goldfinches.

COW PARSLEY

Anthriscus sylvestris

This medium to tall perennial is often found in hedge-banks, rough grass and shady places and has a rather bushy habit. It bears umbels of white flowers from April to June, followed by oblong, smooth fruits which are black or dark brown when ripe. It is ideal for the wild flower garden.
Height: 60–120 cm (2–4 ft).
Cultivation: Prefers well-drained soil and semi-shade. Self-seeds freely.
Benefits: Like other wild flowers, when allowed to seed, cow parsley provides food for birds in autumn.

COURGETTE PLANT

Cucurbita pepo

A common and easily cultivated garden vegetable. There are a number of varieties, including gold courgettes, which look particularly striking and are as tasty as the more familiar green varieties.
Cultivation: Start plants in pots (sow seeds singly, 2.5 cm (1 in) deep) under glass a month before planting out. Dig a hole 30 cm (1 ft) deep and wide for each plant and half fill with decayed manure or garden compost and plant out after the last frosts. Water lavishly every week when flowering starts, and mulch to conserve soil moisture.
Benefits: A vegetable plot is an excellent source of insects and larvae for hungry garden birds.

WOOD CRANESBILL

Geranium sylvaticum

Commonly found in the wild in grassy places and woods, wood cranesbill is a medium to tall perennial that produces 5-petalled, reddish-mauve, often white-centred flowers with prominent stamens from June to September. In autumn the foliage turns takes on a beautiful red colour. Long, pointed, beak-like fruits 'explode' open to release seeds.
Height: 30–60 cm (1–2 ft).
Cultivation: Prefers damp but not waterlogged soil and can tolerate deep shade.
Benefits: This plant attracts pollinating insects including flies and butterflies. Seed-eating birds will also benefit.

CURLED DOCK

Rumex crispus

A renowned invasive weed on arable land, this vigorous perennial has large, smooth leaves with wavy margins and bears dense whorls of greenish, star-shaped flowers from June to October. The flowers are followed by small, leathery, red-brown fruits. It spreads very quickly in gardens.
Height: 1 m (3 ft).
Spread: 15 cm (6 in).
Cultivation: Grow in moderately fertile, well-drained soil in sun.
Benefits: The seeds are eaten by Jackdaws, finches and Reed Buntings.

DAISY

Bellis perennis

A slow-growing, carpet-forming perennial, daisies are considered as weeds on garden lawns, but a range of large- and miniature-flowered cultivated varieties in shades of red, pink or white are grown as biennials, often in garden borders.
Height: 15–20 cm (6–8 in).
Spread: 15–20 cm (6–8 in).

Cultivation: Grows in sun or semi-shade and in fertile, very well-drained soil.
Benefits: When left to seed daisies are enjoyed by garden birds. Certain insect-eating species are attracted by a variety of pollinating insects that visit the flowers.

POET'S DAFFODIL

Narcissus poeticus

The daffodil has long been grown in gardens for its ornamental flowers and there are several varieties and hybrids available. A late-flowering, spring bulb, the fragrant flowers of poet's daffodil are borne at the end of smooth stems and have white petals and a small, shallow, yellow or orange cup with a red rim. Leaves are long, narrow and greyish-green. This plant is ideal for naturalising in moist turf but possibly slow to establish.
Height: 22–42 cm (9–17 in).
Cultivation: Prefers sun or light shade and well-drained soil.
Benefits: The highly colourful flowers attract insects making them a good choice for encouraging birds to your garden.

OXEYE DAISY
Leucanthemum vulgare

A slightly hairy, medium perennial, this wild flower is a familiar sight in grassy meadows and along roadsides where it grows quite vigorously. It has dark green, coarsely toothed leaves and bears daisy-like flower heads with white rays and prominent yellow disc florets singly from May to September. A number of different types of insect are attracted to the flowers, including flies, bees, beetles and butterflies, making the plant an essential part of any wildlife garden.
Height: 30–60 cm (1–2 ft).
Cultivation: Grows in well-drained to dry soil in full sun. Does not tolerate acid soils.
Benefits: The flowers attract a large number of pollinating insects that provide food for various species of birds.

FENNEL
Foeniculum vulgare

This tall, greyish, strong-smelling biennial/perennial is often grown for its aromatic seeds and fragrant, feathery leaves, which have a wonderfully decorative effect in borders and, along with the seeds, can be used for culinary flavouring. Umbels of yellow flowers appear from July to September. In the wild it is mainly found near the sea.

Fennel attracts hoverflies.
Height: 60–120 cm (2–4 ft)
Cultivation: Grow in an open, sunny position, in fertile, well-drained soil. If planting in a herb garden, do not plant near dill as cross-pollination will reduce fennel's seed production.
Benefits: This plant provides food for birds in the form of seeds and insects.

DILL
Anethum graveolens

Commonly found growing in the wild on waste ground, this slender plant is often used for culinary purposes and is ideal for a herb garden. It has aromatic, feathery, light green leaves, yellow flowers in flattened umbels borne from July to September and flattened, winged fruits. Slugs are known to love this plant.
Height: 90 cm (3 ft).
Cultivation: Grow in light, sandy soil in full sun.
Benefits: Seedheads provide food for birds while slugs, which are found on the plant in large numbers, may attract various invertebrate-feeding species.

COMMON EVENING PRIMROSE
Oenothera biennis

Introduced in Europe in the seventeenth century, this biennial is found in the wild on disturbed ground and sand dunes. It is usually grown in gardens for the long succession of profuse, but short-lived, scented, yellow flowers, which open in the evenings from June to September and attract large numbers of insects.
Height: 1 m (3 ft).
Spread: 40 cm (16 in).
Cultivation: Grow in poor to fairly fertile, well-drained soil in full sun.
Benefits: Insects associated with this plant attract warblers. In addition, fruit capsules contain tiny seeds that are enjoyed by various species of bird, including Chaffinch, Brambling, Greenfinch, Goldfinch and Siskin.

BLUE FESCUE

Festuca glauca

Grasses are an interesting feature in a garden, grown mainly as foliage plants to add contrast to borders and rock gardens, although some have attractive flower heads in summer. The blue fescue found growing in gardens is an evergreen, tuft-forming, perennial grass. The narrow leaves are various shades of blue-green to silvery white and the plant bears panicles of spikelets in summer. This plant is useful as edging or ground cover.

Height: 10 cm (4 in).
Spread: 10 cm (4 in).
Cultivation: Grow in full sun in any dry soil.
Benefits: The seed of grasses is a valuable food supply for seed-eating birds, whilst the tufted growth provides a habitat for other types of bird food such as insects and snails.

GRASSES

Stipa spp.

One of a number of *Stipa* species, pheasant grass (*Stipa arundinacea*, illustrated) is an evergreen, tuft-forming, perennial grass. Its narrow, brownish-green leaves become tinged red, bronze, yellow and orange in late summer, and in autumn, decorative, pendent, open panicles of purplish-green flower spikes appear, making it a much valued ornamental planting in any garden.

Height: 1.5 m (5 ft).
Spread: 1.2 m (4 ft).
Cultivation: Grow in full sun in any well-drained soil.
Benefits: Tall grasses are excellent furnishers of seed for seed-eating birds. In addition, they harbour a variety of insects making them a good source of food for birds such as Reed Buntings.

FOXGLOVE

Digitalis purpurea

A familiar sight in woodland, hedgerows, scrub or heaths, foxglove is also commonly cultivated in gardens where a number of different forms and colours are grown. It is a tall, upright plant with spear-shaped leaves, and, in summer, tall spikes of nodding, tubular, sometimes dark-spotted flowers in shades of pink, red, purple or white. The flowers, which are closely set, attract large numbers of bumblebees. Seeds are contained in dry fruit capsules.

Height: 1–1.5 m (3–5 ft).
Spread: 60 cm (2 ft).
Cultivation: Grows in most situations, including dry, exposed sites, but does best in semi-shade and moist, but well-drained soil.
Benefits: The scattered seeds of foxglove are eaten by some birds. Bees attracted to the flowers provide food for insect-eating species such as flycatchers.

GOLDEN ROD

Solidago virgaurea

This invasive, herbaceous perennial, mainly found growing in woods, scrub and on grassland, is well-suited to 'wild gardens' where it is a popular choice for being a late-flowering species. Ideal for the herbaceous border, it spreads rapidly to form dense clumps. Many minute heads of golden-yellow, daisy-like flowers are produced in showy masses on the branching stems among the hoary, sharply pointed leaves. The flowering season is from July to September and the flowers are followed by small, hairy seeds.

Height: 75 cm (2.5 ft).
Spread: 45 cm (1.5 ft).
Cultivation: Grow in poor, preferably sandy, well-drained soil in full sun. Self-seeds easily.
Benefits: The flowers attract pollinating insects, a source of food for some species of birds. Seeds are eaten by Greenfinch, Goldfinch, Siskin and Linnet.

STINKING IRIS   *Iris foetidissima*

This evergreen species is ideal for a bog or water garden. The tall, branched stems bear dull purplish-grey flowers from early to midsummer, while cylindrical seed pods open to reveal rounded, bright orange seeds throughout winter. When crushed, the leaves produce a sickly sweet smell, from which the plant derives its name.
Height: 30 cm–1 m (1–3 ft).
Spread: Indefinite.
Cultivation: Will thrive in a bog or water garden but also tolerates drier conditions.
Benefits: The seeds are eaten by birds.

LORDS AND LADIES, CUCKOO PINT *Arum maculatum*

This perennial of patch-forming habit is commonly found in woods, copses and on shady banks. It is often grown in gardens for its ornamental leaves, which are arrow-shaped, dark green and frequently dark-spotted, and attractive sheaths (spathes), which enclose a finger-like, purple spike (spadix) of tiny flowers. The flowers, which open in April and May are visited by pollinating flies. In late summer the plant bears heads of green, berry-like seeds which turn a striking, bright orange colour as they ripen in early autumn.

Height: 30–60 cm (1–2 ft).
Cultivation: Prefers sun or partial shade, and moist but well-drained soil.
Benefits: The berries are a valuable food source for birds as are pollinating flies which visit the flowers in spring.

COMMON KNAPWEED   *Centaurea nigra*

Common knapweed is found in the wild in rough grassy places, hedgerows and on verges. Also known as black knapweed or hardheads, this perennial is usually grown in gardens for its striking, purple flower heads which are brush-like and borne singly or in clusters, sometimes surrounded by a ring of slender ray petals. The flowers, which appear from June to September, are sought out by a wide range of pollinating insects, including bees and butterflies. Suitable for the 'wild garden'.
Height: 10–60 cm (4 in–2 ft).
Cultivation: Requires sun and any well-drained soil.
Benefits: A variety of insect life can be found on this plant, making it particularly attractive to insect-eating birds. Seeds are enjoyed by finches.

PURPLE LOOSESTRIFE   *Lythrum salicaria*

A tall, colourful, upright plant that thrives at the edge of water, especially river and lake margins, purple loosestrife is ideal for bog gardens. It has hairy, long, narrow leaves that turn red in late summer. From June to August it also bears whorls of closely set, purple-pink flowers on long spires, which are followed by oval fruit capsules containing numerous seeds. This plant self-seeds freely and can become invasive.
Height: 60 cm (2 ft) or more.
Cultivation: Requires full sun or semi-shade and moist or wet soil.
Benefits: The seeds of this wild flower attract many seed-eating birds. Pollinating insects visit the flowers in summer, encouraging the birdlife.

POT MARIGOLD   *Calendula officinalis*

This wild flower mainly grows on waste ground. It is a fast-growing, bushy plant of which there are a number of cultivars for garden planting. The light green, lance-shaped leaves are very aromatic and the plant bears daisy-like, single or double flower heads in orange or yellow colours from spring to autumn. Slugs love the leaves of young marigolds. Self-seeds abundantly.

Height and Spread: Tall cultivars, 60 cm (2 ft); dwarf forms, 30 cm (1 ft).

Cultivation: Grow in sun and in any well-drained soil.

Benefits: The brightly-coloured flowers draw insects to the plant, making it attractive to insect-eating birds.

MARSH MARIGOLD, KINGCUP   *Caltha palustris*

A deciduous perennial that grows at the margins of water. It has rounded or heart-shaped, glossy, dark green leaves against which are contrasted the clusters of cup-shaped, bright yellow flowers in spring. It makes a particularly attractive planting at the edge of a pond.

Height: 60 cm (2 ft).

Spread: 45 cm (1.5 ft).

Cultivation: Plant in boggy ground or very shallow water. Prefers full sun. Ideal for the water garden.

Benefits: The flowers are visited by a variety of pollinating insects, including flies and beetles, attracting birds like the Grey Wagtail which always forages for food near water.

MICHAELMAS DAISY   *Aster x salignus*

Commonly found in the wild in damp and waste places and by streams, Michaelmas daisies are medium to tall perennials. They naturalise well, and are good as a background subject in flower borders. The flowers, which appear in late summer and autumn, have yellow disc florets and purple, violet or whitish rays, and are borne in widely branched clusters.

Height: 30–60 cm (1–2 ft) or more.

Cultivation: Prefers sun or partial shade and fertile, well-drained soil.

Benefits: The flowers attract a large diversity of pollinating insects, including butterflies, moths, flies and beetles. Seeds are eaten by Siskins and other finches.

MASTERWORT   *Astrantia major*

A wild flower of woods and mountain meadows. This medium to tall perennial is commonly cultivated in gardens. It produces umbels of rather pretty, greenish-white, sometimes pink-tinged flowers throughout summer and autumn above a dense mass of divided, mid-green leaves. The flowers attract a wide range of insects and are also much prized by flower arrangers.

Height: 60 cm (2 ft).

Spread: 45 cm (1.5 ft).

Cultivation: Requires sun or semi-shade and moist, well-drained soil.

Benefits: Birds will be encouraged by the insect life associated with this plant.

WATER MINT
Mentha aquatica

A member of the mint family, this pleasantly aromatic perennial grows in wet places, such as around ponds or by streams. Its scent varies from musty mint to strong peppermint. The leaves are mid-green, soft and slightly downy and from July to September it bears small, bell-shaped, lilac or pink-lilac flowers in leafy spikes. Also suitable for container growing.
Height: 10–60 cm (4–24 in).
Cultivation: Grow in water or waterlogged soil, in sun or partial shade.
Benefits: This plant commonly attracts insects making it a useful addition to any wildlife garden and helping to encourage the birds.

GREAT MULLEIN
Verbascum thapsus

Commonly found in the wild in waste places and on roadsides, great mullein is a tall, stout biennial that creates an ideal background subject in a wild flower garden. In its first year the plant consists of a large rosette of leaves covered with a thick, silvery-white, woolly down. Closely-packed, flat, yellow flowers are borne in long, dense spikes in the second summer from June to August. The fruits are small, egg-shaped capsules which split open dispersing numerous tiny seeds.
Height: to 2 m (6 ft).
Cultivation: Prefers an open, sunny position and well-drained soil.
Benefits: Butterflies and other insects are drawn to the flowers in summer. The seed of this wild flower is an attractive feature for seed-eating birds.

CORN POPPY, FIELD POPPY
Papaver rhoeas

A tall, erect annual with distinctive, large, cup-shaped, red flowers, corn poppies grow in fields and on waste land, but are also commonly cultivated in gardens. The flowers are produced from May to July. When they fall they leave behind hard fruit capsules packed with tiny seeds.
Height: 90 cm (3 ft).
Spread: 10 cm (4 in).
Cultivation: Requires sun or semi-shade, and prefers moist, but well-drained soil. Self-seeds easily.
Benefits: Flowers are visited by pollinating insects, including flies and beetles as well as bees, providing food for several species of bird. Dunnocks, Jackdaws, sparrows and finches feed on seeds.

COMMON NETTLE
Urtica doica

This vigorous perennial grows in open country, woods and waste land. The infamous stinging leaves, although sometimes making the plant unpopular with humans, attract caterpillars as well as other insects, making it an essential part of any wildlife garden. The leaves can also be used for culinary purposes. The male and female flowers which are yellowish-green are borne on separate plants. The female flowers hang down in clusters whereas the male flowers stick out.
Height: 1.5 m (5 ft).
Spread: 15 cm (6 in).
Cultivation: Grows in waterlogged or very moist soil in sun or partial shade. Keep in a confined area.
Benefits: Caterpillars are an important food for tits. In addition to the insect life associated with this plant, the seeds also provide food for many birds, including Siskins, Bullfinches and Reed Buntings.

YELLOW-HORNED POPPY
Glaucium flavum

Yellow-horned poppy is a coastal species rarely found inland. It is a slow-growing, erect perennial with wavy-edged, fleshy, greyish-green leaves and solitary, yellow, poppy-like flowers in summer and early autumn. The flowers are followed by long, slender fruit capsules from August to November, which split open to release the seed when ripe.
Height: 30–60 cm (1–2 ft).
Spread: 45 cm (1.5 ft).
Cultivation: Requires full sun and well-drained, non-acidic soil.
Benefits: The flowers are visited by insect pollinators providing benefits for insect-eating species of birds. Seeds released from the mature fruit capsules provide additional food.

SEA HOLLY
Eryngium maritimum

A short to medium perennial ideal for gardens in coastal locations where it is commonly found growing in the wild. It has leathery, spiny, blue-green leaves with whitish veins and tight umbels of powder blue, thistle-like flowers in July and August.

Height: 30–60 cm (1–2 ft).
Cultivation: Grows in well-drained to dry soil, in full sun.
Benefits: Birds may be attracted by pollinating insects, such as flies and beetles, which visit the flowers in summer.

PRIMROSE
Primula vulgaris

A common and widespread wild flower found growing in woodland, grassy banks, ditches and on cliffs, the primrose has been widely hybridised in gardens. It has long been regarded as the herald of spring, its common name deriving from the Latin *prima rosa*, meaning the first flower. A low-growing, clump-forming perennial, the scented, soft yellow flowers are borne singly among oval- to lance-shaped, bright green leaves in spring. Seeds are shed from the shrivelled flower heads at the end of the summer.
Height: 15–20 cm (6–8 in).
Spread: 15–20 cm (6–8 in).
Cultivation: Prefers partial shade and moist but well-drained soil.
Benefits: A wide diversity of insect food, including bees, butterflies and slugs, are associated with garden primroses encouraging the presence of insectivorous birds in your garden. Chaffinches eat the seeds.

FLOWERING RUSH
Butomus umbellatus

This evergreen perennial grows in shallow water and pond margins. Its long, narrow, rush-like leaves change colour as they mature, from mid-green, through bronze-purple, to dark green. Umbels of bright pink flowers appear from July to August.

Height: 1 m (3 ft).
Spread: 45 cm (18 in).
Cultivation: Grow in water (water depth can vary between 5 and 25 cm (2 and 10 in). Requires full sun.
Benefits: Birds are attracted to this plant by insects and use leaves for cover.

SOLOMON'S SEAL

Polygonatum multiflorum

A popular garden plant, solomon's seal is a graceful, arching, leafy perennial. In late spring it produces drooping clusters of bell-shaped, greenish-white flowers held close to the stem at the base of the oval to lance-shaped mid-green leaves. The flowers are followed by handsome, spherical, green berries that ripen to a blue-black colour. Sawfly caterpillar is commonly found on the plant.
Height: 30–60 cm (1–2 ft).
Cultivation: Requires a cool, shady position and fertile, well-drained soil.
Benefits: Berries provide a welcome food source for birds, while insects, in particular caterpillars, which are attractive to tits, are often found on the plant.

STONECROP

Sedum spp.

Sedum is a large genus of fleshy or succulent, erect or prostrate plants, suitable for various purposes, for example in mixed borders, rock gardens or as carpet bedding. Pictured here is *Sedum spectabile*, commonly known as ice plant. Above the mounds of fleshy, grey-green leaves, star-shaped, pink flowers that attract bees and butterflies are borne in late summer and autumn. Because of its greater height, this species is best for the mixed border.
Height: 45 cm (1.5 ft).
Spread: 45 cm (1.5 ft).
Cultivation: Requires sun. *Sedum spectabile* will thrive even in poor, drought-prone soils.
Benefits: Birds may benefit from the insect life associated with the plant, in particular flycatchers, which will eat bees and butterflies.

TUFTED SEDGE

Carex elata

Sedges add an interesting element to gardens at the same time as being beneficial to the birdlife. Some grow naturally in water, making a good choice for a water garden, but many may be grown in any well-drained soil. Tufted sedge is an evergreen, perennial that forms large tussocks and is suitable for growing in gardens with ponds. It has triangular stems which bear long, narrow leaves and in summer blackish-brown spikelets of flowers.
Height: to 60 cm (2 ft).
Spread: 20 cm (8 in).
Cultivation: Grow in water or waterlogged soil at pond margins, in sun or partial shade.
Benefits: Insects and seeds are an important attraction of this plant for birds. In addition, they can seek cover in the tufted growth.

TEASEL

Dipsacus fullonum

Teasel is a tall biennial or short-lived perennial herb, with a rosette of large leaves, and a prickly stem carrying an egg-shaped, spiny head of tiny, purple flowers that appear in July and August and attract a variety of pollinating insects. Started from seed, teasel is ideal for the wild flower garden and the seedheads, which last until November, provide wonderful winter decoration.
Height: 2 m (6 ft 6 in).
Spread: 60 cm (2 ft).
Cultivation: Grows in moderately fertile soil, in sun or part-shade.
Benefits: A seed-bearing plant, teasel is good for attracting Goldfinches in late summer and autumn, as well as sparrows and buntings. The flowers are visited by pollinating insects an added benefit for the birds visiting your garden.

SUNFLOWER

Helianthus annuus

Often cultivated as a crop, the sunflower is a native North American plant. It can be invasive and is sometimes found growing in the wild on waste land. Several horticultural forms have been developed and are ideal for borders or background subjects in gardens. *Helianthus annuus* 'Teddy Bear' (illustrated) is a dwarf cultivar and has wide, fully double, deep yellow flower heads on tall stems.

Height: 60 cm (2 ft).
Cultivation: Sunflowers require full sun and moderately fertile, moist but well-drained soil. Support flowers with stakes.
Benefits: The flower heads, which are packed with seeds, furnish a valuable food supply for many birds including Collared Doves, Waxwings, Long-tailed Tits, crows, Nuthatches and Greenfinches.

WELTED THISTLE

Carduus acanthoides

Commonly found on waste land, verges and in hedgerows and usually considered as weeds, a number of thistle species are cultivated for their flower heads and foliage. This medium to tall, prickly biennial has purple flowers that attract bees and butterflies from June to August, followed by ripe seeds in September.
Height: 1.2 m (4 ft).
Spread: 50 cm (17 in).
Cultivation: Grows in full sun in well-drained soil. Self-seeds freely and can become invasive.
Benefits: As well as providing seeds for birds such as Greenfinches, Goldfinches and Siskins, thistles attract a variety of insect life.

TICKSEED

Coreopsis spp.

Tickseeds are often grown for their colourful, daisy-like flower heads and their long season of garden decoration, blooming from early summer to frost. *Coreopsis grandiflora* (illustrated) has leafy stems and solitary heads with bright yellow ray flowers. Tickseeds make excellent cut flowers.
Height: 45–120 cm (1.5–4 ft).
Cultivation: Require full sun and fertile, well-drained soil.
Benefits: The flowers provide a mass of colour attracting many insects, in turn encouraging bird activity in your garden.

WATERCRESS   *Rorippa nasturtium-aquaticum*

Watercress is found growing in and by shallow, flowing water. It is a creeping perennial with pinnate leaves, white flowers from May to October, and seed pods held horizontally. The plant has culinary uses.

Height: 10–60 cm (4–24 in).
Cultivation: Grows in water in full sun.
Benefits: Seeds provide food for birds.

WOODRUFF   *Galium odoratum*

Commonly found growing in the wild in woods, this is an aromatic, carpet-forming perennial that bears whorls of star-shaped, white flowers above the prickly, whorled leaves in summer. The flowers attract bees and flies. Woodruff is good for growing in the dry shade of trees.

Height: 15 cm (6 in).
Spread: 30 cm (1 ft) or more.
Cultivation: Prefers part shade and well-drained, rich, alkaline soil.
Benefits: Insect-eating species, such as flycatchers, Swifts, Swallows and House Martins, are attracted by flying insect-pollinators that visit the flowers in summer.

WHITE WATERLILY   *Nymphaea alba*

A deciduous perennial, this floating water plant will add an attractive splash of colour to a garden pond, as well as providing benefits for the birdlife. The cup-shaped, pure white flowers with golden centres appear in summer.

Spread: to 3 m (10 ft).
Cultivation: Requires an open, sunny position and still water.
Benefits: Birds are attracted to this plant by insects commonly found on it, especially pollinating flies.

YARROW   *Achillea millefolium*

This perennial is commonly found in hedgerows, grassland, meadows and on roadsides. It has long been cultivated in gardens in various colour forms, being particularly well-suited to wild flower and rock gardens. Yarrow has finely-divided, fern-like foliage, which is strongly aromatic when bruised, and produces clusters of tiny, whitish-pink flowers from June to November. The flowers are visited by a wide variety of insects including bees, flies and butterflies.
Height: 60 cm (2 ft)

Spread: 60 cm (2 ft).
Cultivation: Requires moist, well-drained soil in full sun. Grow in an open site or container. Will tolerate drought conditions so does well in coastal locations.
Benefits: Seedheads provide food for several species of birds, including tits, House Sparrows, Chaffinches, Greenfinches and Bullfinches, while aphids and pollinating insects commonly found on the plant attract a variety of insect-eating birds.

Bird Directory

The Bird Directory has been designed to help you identify the different species of birds most likely to visit gardens throughout Britain, and gives useful information on their individual behaviour and life cycles. Being able to recognise each species means you will gain greater enjoyment from the wildlife in your garden, and, more importantly, will know exactly how to cater for the birds' particular requirements.

In addition to key identification features such as size, plumage, jizz and flight silhouettes, for each bird there is also a brief description of its song or call, so that it can be identified by sound as well as sight. An explanation of which parts of the country and at what times of the year each species is usually found, will help confirm an identification. The bird descriptions also give a detailed summary of each species' habits, for example whether it is a nocturnal species or is usually seen by day, where it is usually seen and how it behaves, in addition to information on its feeding and breeding habits.

Each description is accompanied by illustrations of the birds in different plumages, as well as by a distribution map to aid identification.

KEY TO MAPS

Summer visitor only

Winter visitor only

Resident
(all the year round)

GREY HERON
Ardea cinerea

Generally the largest wild bird to visit gardens, the Grey Heron is a wily predator, often seizing fish from garden ponds. It may also be seen flying overhead, appearing as a huge, dark silhouette.

Identification features: 90–100 cm (36–40 in). A very large, upright bird, with a long, curved neck and long legs. At a distance appears mainly grey, but closer views reveal a thick black stripe on the head and paler underparts streaked with black. Herons have a sharp, pointed, yellow bill, perfect for spearing their prey. Juveniles lack the black markings on the head. In flight appears huge, with long, broad wings, long legs and a curved neck.

Song and calls: A loud, deep note, often said to sound like 'fraaank!'

Where and when: Herons can be found throughout Britain and Ireland, though they are commoner near the coast or large rivers, and generally absent from mountainous regions. Present throughout the year, but perhaps more likely to visit gardens during the winter, especially when harsh weather causes lakes and ponds to freeze.

Habits: Herons generally visit gardens early or late in the day, as they are shy birds and prefer to avoid human contact. If you have a garden pond, herons may regularly come to steal fish; otherwise, they are most likely to be seen in flight overhead.

Feeding: Herons feed on a wide variety of aquatic animals, especially fish and frogs. In cold weather, when their normal prey is hard to find, they may also take rodents and small birds.

Breeding: Herons nest in large, communal colonies known as heronries, sometimes starting to breed as early as January. They lay four to five pale blue eggs, and incubate for 25–26 days. Young leave the nest about three weeks later.

adult

adult summer

immature

MALLARD
Anas platyrhynchos

adult male

adult female

adult female

adult male

adult male eclipse

The most widespread, commonest and best known wild duck in Britain and Europe, the Mallard is an occasional visitor to larger gardens, especially those near water.

Identification features: 51–62 cm (20–24 in). The male is easy to identify, with his bottle-green head, thin white collar, yellow bill and deep purplish-brown breast. The female is mainly brown, with dark centres to the feathers giving a mottled appearance. On the edge of the wing, both male and female have a blue 'speculum' bordered with white. During late summer Mallards undergo a prolonged moult, during which males resemble females, in a plumage known as 'eclipse'.

Song and calls: The classic 'quack' is uttered only by the female; the male has a low, soft whistling call.

Where and when: Found virtually throughout Britain, though less abundant in south-west England, Wales and north-west Scotland. Also common in parts of Ireland, though has a patchier distribution there. Resident, so present throughout the year, though may be harder to see during the annual moult in late summer.

Habits: Mallards are brash, confiding birds, always the first to come to feed on scraps of bread. They generally prefer open areas of water with surrounding vegetation, but are adaptable enough to visit garden ponds and lawns to feed.

Feeding: In their natural habitat Mallards feed on a variety of aquatic animals and plants, mainly by dabbling with their bill just below the water surface. However, they will also feed on kitchen scraps, especially bread.

Breeding: Mallards breed early, sometimes having eggs by February in southern England. Lays 9–12 cream-coloured or buffish eggs, which they incubate for four weeks. The fluffy young leave the nest as soon as they are born, and fledge between seven and eight weeks later. One brood.

SPARROWHAWK

Accipiter brevipes

Shy but widespread, the Sparrowhawk is second only to the Kestrel as Britain's commonest bird of prey. Most often seen as it flies low over gardens in search of its songbird prey.

Identification features: 28–38 cm (11–15 in). The sparrowhawk is generally seen in flight, where its stocky shape, rounded wings and long tail tell it apart from the more slender-winged Kestrel. It also has a characteristic habit of alternating a series of wing flaps with short glides. Like many birds of prey, the female is considerably larger than the male, and is dark brown above and pale below, with a characteristic streak above the eye. The smaller male is bluish above, with underparts streaked orange and white.

Song and calls: Sometimes utters a penetrating, high-pitched 'kew-kew-kew'.

Where and when: In recent years the Sparrowhawk has made a comeback, mainly as a result of the banning of harmful agricultural pesticides such as DDT. Now found across much of Britain and Ireland, though absent from much of north and west Scotland. Commonest in gardens with plenty of trees and bushes, which it can use as cover and a place to nest. Resident, present throughout the year.

Habits: A shy, sometimes elusive bird, often preferring to keep low or concealed in thick foliage. Hunts by flying fast and low, using an element of surprise to ambush small birds, which are rapidly dispatched with its sharp talons.

Feeding: Sparrowhawks feed almost entirely on small songbirds, often taken while they are feeding on bird tables or feeding stations.

adult male

adult female

juvenile

adult

juvenile

Breeding: Sparrowhawks nest from April to July, coinciding with the peak numbers of songbirds to feed their hungry young. They lay between three and six pale bluish-white eggs with brown smudges, which they incubate for four to five weeks. The young fledge three or four weeks later. One brood.

BUZZARD

Buteo buteo

Britain's largest common bird of prey, the Buzzard may be seen soaring on broad wings, especially during fine, sunny weather. In recent years the species has begun to spread out from its western strongholds to eastern parts of the country.

Identification features: 51–57 cm (20–22 in). A large, broad-winged bird of prey, generally seen in flight. Usually dark brown, though plumage varies considerably, and birds may appear very pale or dark below. Closer views reveal that the wings are tipped with black, contrasting with the paler underwings and darker brown 'shoulders'. On the ground, the dark brown plumage and large hooked bill are distinctive.

Song and calls: A far-carrying 'mewing' sound.

Where and when: Commonest in the northern and western parts of Britain, where it is often associated with upland areas. However, thanks to the banning

of agricultural chemicals and a drop in persecution, Buzzards are now spreading eastwards, and may be seen in small numbers in formerly unoccupied areas. Also found in Northern Ireland, but virtually absent from the Republic. Resident, present throughout the year.

Habits: Like most large birds of prey, the Buzzard prefers warm, sunny weather, which enables it to soar on thermal air currents. Generally confined to wooded areas, though in Wales and south-west England frequently seen over towns.

Feeding: Generally feeds on small mammals, especially rodents, but will also take small birds and carrion.

Breeding: Buzzards build a large, untidy nest on trees or occasionally cliffs. They lay two to four white eggs, blotched with reddish-brown, which they incubate for about five weeks. The young fledge seven to eight weeks later. One brood.

adult dark

adult pale

adult dark

KESTREL

Falco tinnunculus

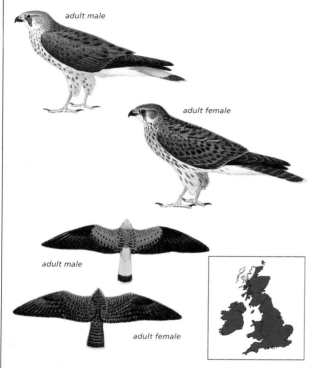

adult male

adult female

adult male

adult female

Our commonest and most familiar bird of prey, the Kestrel is usually seen as it hovers motionless in the air, its keen eyes searching for prey on the ground below.

Identification features: 32–36 cm (13–14 in). A slender, graceful falcon, with long, tapered wings. Generally seen in flight, either hovering or dashing past at speed. The male is a handsome bird, with blue-grey head, rusty upperparts spotted with black, paler underparts spotted with black, dark wingtips and tail. The female is larger and bulkier, with reddish-orange upperparts and buffish underparts, both heavily streaked with black. Perches in an upright position.

Song and calls: High-pitched, repetitive 'kee-kee-kee'.

Where and when: Found throughout most of Britain and Ireland, absent only from Shetland and parts of north-west Scotland, though generally scarcer in western areas.

Kestrels are well-adapted to a wide variety of urban and rural habitats, and can be found in the heart of towns and cities as well as the countryside. Resident, present throughout the year.

Habits: An opportunistic hunter, Kestrels may be seen searching for prey, often hovering virtually stationary above a grassy verge. Not as regular a garden visitor as the Sparrowhawk, as it prefers to hunt in more open country.

Feeding: Preys mainly on small rodents, especially voles, but will also take small birds and occasionally insects or amphibians.

Breeding: Usually nests in a hole in a tree, or in urban areas, on the roof of a building. Will also nest in specially-designed nestboxes. Breeds from March to July, laying three to six pale eggs blotched reddish-brown, which it incubates for four weeks. The young fledge four to five weeks later. One brood.

PHEASANT

Phasianus colchicus

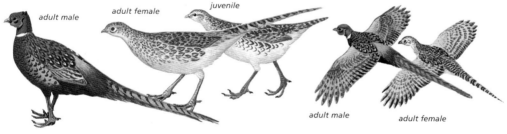

adult male

adult female

juvenile

adult male

adult female

Our largest common gamebird, the male pheasant is also one of our most handsome birds. Originally introduced from south-west Asia by the Romans, it is now widely reared for shooting.

Identification features: 52–90 cm (20–35 in). With his rusty plumage, long tail and brightly-coloured face-pattern, the male Pheasant is unmistakable. However, plumages vary considerably, with birds appearing darker or paler than normal, and many showing a white collar. In contrast, the female is smaller and much duller than the male, her brown, streaked plumage providing camouflage against predators.

Song and calls: A deep, harsh, far-carrying croak; often heard at dawn or dusk.

Where and when: Found throughout much of Britain and Ireland, though absent from Shetland, most of north-west Scotland and parts of central and southern Wales. Resident, present throughout the year, though more likely to visit gardens during the winter.

Habits: Depending on whether shooting takes place nearby, the Pheasant can either be very shy and elusive, or extraordinarily tame, even feeding from the hand! Prefers to feed close to the woodland edge, but may also be found in gardens, especially those in lowland rural areas.

Feeding: Adults feed mainly on the shoots of arable farmland crops, but will also take a variety of plant and invertebrate food, obtained by scratching or digging the ground. Young feed mainly on small insects.

Breeding: Nests in a small hollow on the ground, usually amongst vegetation to provide cover against predators. Lays large clutches of between seven and seventeen pale green eggs, which it incubates for three or four weeks. The young can walk as soon as they hatch, and fly twelve days later. One brood.

MOORHEN

Gallinula chloropus

Mainly found on or near water, the Moorhen will sometimes visit gardens in order to feed. Although it superficially resembles a small duck, it is in fact a member of the rail family, like its close relative the Coot.

Identification features: 31–35 cm (12–14 in). A medium-sized, dumpy-looking water bird, with dark bluish-black head and underparts and dark brown upperparts, separated by a narrow white line. When swimming or walking shows a distinctive white undertail, which it jerks in a highly distinctive manner. Legs are dull greenish-yellow; the bill is red, with a bright yellow tip. Juvenile Moorhens are basically dull brown with a buff undertail and plain brown bill.

Song and calls: Gives a variety of calls, including a loud, explosive kerr-ukk, and a repetitive 'ki-ki-ki-ki-kik'.

Where and when: Found on almost any lowland fresh water throughout England, Wales, Ireland and southern Scotland, and in smaller numbers as far north as Orkney and Shetland. Largely absent from north and west Scotland. Resident, present throughout the year. Moorhens often visit gardens during harsh winter weather, when snow and ice make their usual food supply unobtainable.

Habits: A rather shy bird, Moorhens often keep close to vegetation, so may not always be seen immediately. In gardens near water they may visit lawns to feed.

Feeding: Moorhens take a wide range of small aquatic invertebrates, and will also feed on land, especially areas of damp grass.

Breeding: Builds a compact, floating nest, usually near vegetation at the edge of the water. Clutch size varies enormously, though averages about seven. The downy young hatch after three weeks, and swim immediately, fledging six or seven weeks later. May have several broods.

juvenile

adult

adult

COMMON GULL

Larus canus

A regular autumn and winter visitor to much of the country, the Common Gull is a handsome and distinctive bird. Although shyer than its smaller relative the Black-headed Gull, it will often visit gardens in search of food.

Identification features: 38–43 cm (15–17 in). Given good views, easily distinguished from Black-headed Gull by its noticeably larger size, plumper shape, plain white head and yellow-green bill. It can be told apart from larger gulls such as Herring and Lesser Black-backed by size, bill and leg colour. In flight, the rounded wings with obvious black wingtips are distinctive. Juveniles and immatures have varying amounts of brown on the wings, and a dark band across the tail.

Song and calls: High-pitched, penetrating scream.

Where and when: Mainly confined as a breeding bird to northern Britain, where it nests in large, noisy colonies. From midsummer, the first birds begin to move south, and by autumn they may be present in large flocks, often on school playing fields or parks. During autumn and winter they frequently visit gardens in search of food to scavenge. Non-breeding birds may be present in small numbers throughout the year.

Habits: Like all gulls, forms mixed flocks which explore an area in search of food, soon gathering in large numbers when they find some. Often perches on roofs, before swooping down to snatch a morsel. As dusk approaches, will fly off to a nearby lake or reservoir to roost.

Feeding: Like most gulls, will eat almost anything, including bread and kitchen scraps.

Breeding: Breeds in colonies, away from gardens.

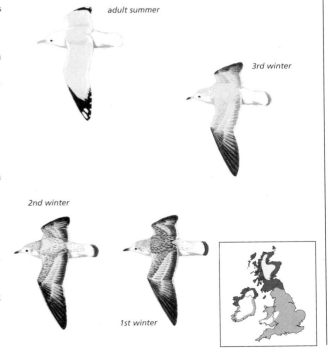

adult summer

3rd winter

2nd winter

1st winter

BLACK-HEADED GULL

Larus ridibundus

By far the commonest and most familiar gull in most parts of the country, especially inland areas, where they are a common sight during the autumn and winter months. In recent years Black-headed Gulls have adapted to living alongside human beings, taking full advantage of our wastefulness.

Identification features: 35–38 cm (14–15 in). Most likely to be seen in non-breeding plumage, when the only remnant of the 'black head' is a small, dark spot behind the eye. Otherwise a small, rather slender gull, with a pale grey back and white underparts, and long, narrow wings giving a rather slim appearance. From late winter some birds begin to moult into breeding plumage, revealing a dark chocolate-brown hood. In flight, the narrow, pointed wings with pale primaries and a dark edge to the wingtips are distinctive.

Young birds show large amounts of brown on wings and tail.

Song and calls: Gives a variety of loud, noisy, wailing calls.

Where and when: A frequent visitor to gardens throughout Britain and Ireland, though far commoner from late summer until the following spring, when most depart north to breed. However, non-breeding birds may be seen in smaller numbers throughout the year.

Habits: A sociable bird, often found in large, noisy flocks. Black-headed Gulls appear to be more used to humans than many other species of gull, and will usually be the first to arrive when there's food available. After feeding, they often gather in flocks on open areas of grass such as playing fields.

Feeding: Like other gulls, feeds on a wide variety of items, including food provided by humans. Will always come to bread, and is able to catch

pieces in mid-air: always an entertaining sight!

Breeding: Nests in large, noisy colonies, though some will continue to visit nearby gardens for food during the breeding season.

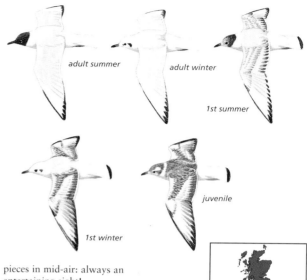

adult summer

adult winter

1st summer

1st winter

juvenile

STOCK DOVE

Columba oenas

Often overlooked, the Stock Dove is in fact widely, if thinly, spread across much of central and southern Britain. Stock Doves are hole-nesters, and often found in gardens with large, mature trees.

Identification features: 32–34 cm (13 in). Smaller and more delicate-looking than the Wood Pigeon, which it superficially resembles. Plumage mainly steel-grey, with a pinkish-mauve wash on the breast, a greenish sheen on the side of the neck, dark tail and wingtips. The bill

is yellowish, and the legs pink. In flight, can generally be told apart from the Wood Pigeon by the lack of white on the neck and wing, though be wary of confusion with the young of that species.

Song and calls: A deep, soft, repetitive pair of notes, repeated a number of times.

Where and when: Common and widespread throughout England, Wales and southern Scotland, with small numbers on the Scottish east coast as far north as Loch Ness. Also found

in Ireland, mainly in the east and south. Resident, present throughout the year.

Habits: A shy bird, very different from its brasher relatives. Often perches quietly on the branch of a tree, flying when disturbed. Easiest to see in late winter and early spring, when pairs perform their courtship flight, flying around together and clapping their wings.

Feeding: Like most pigeons and doves, feeds mainly on seeds, which it takes from the ground by pecking.

Breeding: Stock Doves have a long breeding season, beginning as early as February and continuing into late autumn. Generally nests in a hole in a tree, where it lays two white eggs, which are incubated for 16–18 days. The young are born helpless, and fledge about three to four weeks later. Stock Doves have several broods, with up to five recorded.

adult

juvenile

adult

FERAL PIGEON

Columba livia

adult

juvenile

feral variants

adult

One of our most familiar yet most ignored birds, the Feral Pigeon is surely the most successful species this century. Originally descended from the wild Rock Dove, domesticated for food and sport, Feral Pigeons have spread throughout the country, with the population continuing to increase at a phenomenal rate.
Identification features: 31–34 cm (12–13 in). Very variable: coming in a whole range of shades and colours from almost pure white, through browns and greys, to virtually black.

The 'typical' bird mimics its wild ancestor, with a mainly steel-grey plumage, two black wingbars and a pale rump.
Song and calls: Familiar cooing noise, usually uttered in groups of three notes.
Where and when: Feral Pigeons are found in cities, towns, suburbs and rural areas throughout most of lowland Britain, though in the northern and western isles they are still outnumbered by wild Rock Doves. Resident, present throughout the year.
Habits: A sociable bird, usually

seen in small parties of ten or twenty birds, and occasionally in much larger flocks. Attracted by the presence of food, and may gather in noisy groups on nearby roofs before coming down into a garden to feed. Noisy and quarrelsome.
Feeding: The ultimate feeding machine: eating almost anything edible (and occasionally inedible) with gusto. Artificial feeding can cause problems of noise and danger to public health, so it is generally not a good idea to encourage the species.

Breeding: Breeds all year round, raising as many as six broods, especially where food is plentiful. Lays two white eggs, which hatch between two and three weeks later. The young fledge after four or five weeks.

WOOD PIGEON

Columba palumbus

The Wood Pigeon is a highly adaptable bird, living alongside humans in towns, cities and villages throughout Britain and Ireland. It is by far our commonest pigeon or dove, with more than three million breeding pairs.
Identification features: 40–42 cm (16 in). Given good views, unmistakable. Our largest and bulkiest pigeon, with a distinctive white collar, bordered with green. Plumage basically grey, though shading to pinkish-mauve on the neck and underparts, and warmer-toned on back. Wingtips and tail darker grey; bill orange-yellow; feet and legs yellow. Juvenile birds are paler, and lack the white collar. In flight shows distinctive white bars across wings, distinguishing it from all its relatives.
Song and calls: One of the best-known sounds of town and countryside: a five-syllabled, rather monotonous 'coo-COO

adult

juvenile

adult

coo, coo-coo', with the stress on the second note.
Where and when: Found throughout Britain and Ireland, apart from a few upland areas of Scotland and parts of the Western Isles and Shetland. Resident, present throughout the year.
Habits: A common and regular visitor to gardens large and small, in urban, suburban and rural areas. However, Wood Pigeons are shy and nervous birds, easily frightened off by noise or the appearance of humans.

Feeding: Mainly feeds on seeds, berries and green shoots. Wood Pigeons will feed by clinging onto foliage, visiting bird tables, or taking food from the ground.
Breeding: Breeds throughout the year, even in autumn and winter where conditions are suitable. Builds an untidy nest out of sticks, laying two plain white eggs, which it incubates for 16–17 days. The young fledge three to five weeks later. Usually has two broods.

COLLARED DOVE

Streptopelia decaocto

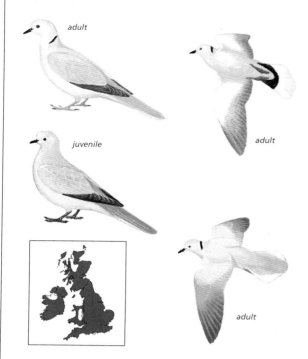

The Collared Dove is one of the most successful species in history, having spread right across Europe from Asia in less than half a century. Nowadays the species is a common and familiar sight – and sound – in many parts of the country.

Identification features: 31–33 cm (12–13 in). A slim, medium-sized, rather pale dove, with a pinkish-buff plumage and distinctive black collar on the sides and back of its neck. Wingtips and tail dark grey; legs and bill grey; eye beady and black. In flight shows dark wings and white tips to the tail-feathers, which contrast with the rest of the plumage.

Song and calls: A repetitive, three-note 'cooo-COOO-coo', with the emphasis on the second syllable.

Where and when: A common visitor to gardens in most suburban and rural areas, though rarely in city centres. Found throughout lowland Britain, but more patchily distributed in Ireland. In recent years the species' spread has begun to slow down, perhaps even beginning to retreat in some parts of the country. Resident, present throughout the year.

Habits: An adaptable and confident bird, frequently perching on roofs or other prominent posts, or feeding on lawns. Often seen in pairs.

Feeding: Collared Doves feed mainly on grain and seeds, found either in gardens or on farms.

Breeding: Mainly breeds from February to October, but has been known to nest all year round. Lays two white eggs, which it incubates for between 14 and 18 days. Young fledge two to three weeks later. Multiple-brooded, with up to five clutches in a single year.

TURTLE DOVE

Streptopelia turtur

Our smallest species of dove, the Turtle Dove has recently suffered a rapid population decline, mainly due to modern farming methods. It gets it name from its haunting, purring call.

Identification features: 26–28 cm (10–11 in). Noticeably smaller than other pigeons or doves, though given poor views it may be confused with its close relative the Collared Dove. The Turtle Dove's dark, mottled upperparts contrast with its plainer, pale pinkish-buff head and underparts. Has a distinctive mark on both sides of the neck, with alternate stripes of black and white, though this may sometimes be hard to see at a distance. On the ground its short legs give it a distinctive 'shuffling' gait. Flight fast and direct, with obvious dark underwings and slim build.

Song and calls: Song a low, rather repetitive purring sound, 'turr-turr-turr', which gives the species its name.

Where and when: A summer visitor to the British Isles, arriving in late April or early May, and departing by September. Virtually confined to lowland farming areas of southern, central and eastern England, with a few pairs in Wales and occasionally Scotland and Ireland. Population and range have seriously declined in recent years, especially in the north and west.

Habits: A shy, sometimes elusive bird, often only given away by its distinctive call. Once seen, often flies away in alarm. Only an occasional visitor to gardens in rural farming areas.

Feeding: Feeds almost entirely on weed seeds and grain, taken on the ground.

Breeding: Breeds from May onwards, building a well-concealed nest from sticks, usually in a hawthorn or elder. Lays one or two white eggs, which it incubates for two weeks. The young fledge three weeks later. Often raises two or even three broods.

CUCKOO

Cuculus canorus

adult male

adult female rufous

juvenile

large fledgling

Of all our summer visitors, the Cuckoo surely has the best-known song; yet the bird itself is rarely seen during its short stay with us. Its other claim to fame is its habit of laying its eggs in other birds nests, and letting them raise its young.

Identification features: 32–34 cm (13 in). More often heard than seen. In flight its slim build, long wings and tail and low, direct flight make it confusable with a falcon or hawk. Also perches on posts and wires, in a horizontal posture with its tail raised. Most birds have steel-grey head, neck and chest, black-and-white barred underparts, and greyish-brown upperparts and tail. However, females also sometimes occur in a rufous phase, similar to female Kestrel.

Song and calls: The male's famous 'Cuck-ooo' song is unmistakable, while the female gives a soft, low bubbling call.

Where and when: A summer visitor to rural areas of Britain and Ireland, thinly but widely distributed throughout. Arrives late April or early May, and adults depart as early as June or July, with young leaving a month or so later.

Habits: Lays its eggs in other birds nests, parasitising a variety of species including Dunnock, Reed Warbler and Meadow Pipit. When males arrive in spring they are easy to see, but soon become elusive.

Feeding: Mainly eats the larvae of butterflies and moths, especially hairy caterpillars! Females are also thought to eat the eggs of their host species.

Breeding: After mating, female cuckoos lay a single egg in up to 25 different nests, each female faithful to a single host species. Before laying, she removes a single egg from the nest, and her own egg is usually camouflaged to resemble that of the host species. The young hatch after 11–13 days, and immediately eject the other eggs and chicks from the nest. The Cuckoo chick fledges between 17 and 21 days later.

ROSE-RINGED (RING-NECKED) PARAKEET

Psittacula krameri

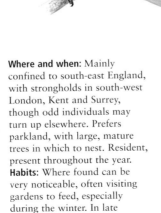

adult male

juvenile

adult female

This gaudy parakeet, originally from Asia, was introduced into southern England in the early 1970s, probably via escapes from the cagebird trade. Since then the species has thrived, its numbers growing spectacularly, though its range still remains fairly limited.

Identification features: 38–42 cm (15–17 in). The only bright emerald-green bird ever likely to be seen in the wild in Britain, although beware other parrot species, which occasionally escape. The Rose-ringed Parakeet's bright, emerald-green plumage, long tail and rose-red bill are distinctive. The male also has the black collar, edged with pink, which gives the species its alternative names. The female's collar is less distinct. In the air appears incredibly slim, with long, narrow wings and tail, and a very rapid, direct flight.

Song and calls: A variety of high-pitched, raucous screeches, often uttered in flight.

Where and when: Mainly confined to south-east England, with strongholds in south-west London, Kent and Surrey, though odd individuals may turn up elsewhere. Prefers parkland, with large, mature trees in which to nest. Resident, present throughout the year.

Habits: Where found can be very noticeable, often visiting gardens to feed, especially during the winter. In late afternoon birds gather together and fly to a communal roost.

Feeding: In its native India, feeds mainly on seeds and soft fruit, but in Britain has taken to visiting artificial bird-feeders, and is especially partial to monkey nuts (peanuts in shells).

Breeding: Nests in holes or cavities in trees, laying 2–4 white eggs, which it incubates for 22–24 days. The young fledge six to seven weeks later. Has also been known to use nestboxes. One, sometimes two, broods.

BARN OWL

Tyto alba

adult light

adult light

adult dark

The quintessential bird of rural Britain, the Barn Owl has suffered a major population decline in recent years. However, thanks to encouragement by farmers, and the use of nestboxes, this magnificent hunter is now making a slow but steady comeback.

Identification features: 33–39 cm (13–15 in). Generally seen at dawn or dusk, when its pale plumage and silent, floating flight give the Barn Owl a mysterious, ghost-like appearance. Distinguished from all other owls by its pale plumage, heart-shaped face and distinctive flight action, holding its wings up as it glides low over the ground. Upperparts golden-buff, delicately marked with tiny spots. Underparts usually white, though may also appear buffish.

Song and calls: Generally silent, but may sometimes utter a short, sharp screech of alarm, the origin of the local name 'Screech Owl'.

Where and when: Patchily distributed across rural parts of England, Wales, and southern Scotland, with a few birds in northern Scotland and Ireland. Strongholds are East Anglia and southern England. Resident, present throughout the year.

Habits: Mainly nocturnal, though also hunts at dawn and dusk, especially during the autumn and winter. Prefers to hunt over open ground, often choosing damp or marshy areas.

Feeding: Feeds almost entirely on rodents, especially voles and mice. Finds prey by sound, using its specially-developed hearing.

Breeding: As its name suggests, breeds mainly in barns or other farm buildings, though will readily take to nestboxes. Lays between four and seven white eggs, which hatch four to five weeks later. Young stay in nest for seven to twelve weeks before fledging. One, sometimes two, broods.

LITTLE OWL

Athene noctua

Our smallest owl, hardly bigger than a Starling. Many people are surprised to learn that the Little Owl was artificially introduced into Britain during the nineteenth century, since when it has spread throughout England and Wales, thriving in rural areas.

Identification features: 21–23 cm (8–9 in). Given good views, its small size and staring yellow eyes make the Little Owl unmistakable. Upperparts dark brownish-grey, with large white spots; underparts paler, heavily streaked and spotted with brown. Crown brown, spotted with white. Distinctive white eyebrows giving a rather stern appearance. Huge claws, with heavily feathered legs. In flight, short, rounded wings and plump body are noticeable.

Song and calls: Song a rather monotonous, far-carrying 'koo-ikk'. Also variety of other mewing and yelping calls.

Where and when: More or less confined to England and Wales, where widely spread throughout lowland rural areas, though rare or absent from parts of south-west England and Wales. Rare in Scotland and absent from Ireland. Resident, present all year round.

Habits: The most diurnal of all our owls, though still most likely to be seen at dawn or dusk. Often perches on a prominent branch, post or building. May visit gardens in rural areas.

Feeding: Feeds on a wide variety of prey, including earthworms, small mammals, birds and insects.

Breeding: Breeds from March onwards, nesting in a tree-hole or cavity in a building. Lays three to five white eggs, which hatch three to four weeks later. Young leave the nest early on, but fledge some weeks later. One brood.

adult

adult

TAWNY OWL

Strix aluco

Our commonest and most widespread owl, its nocturnal habits mean that the Tawny Owl is rarely seen. However, its famous 'tu-whit, tu-whoo' sound is familiar to everyone.

Identification features: A medium-sized owl with a round face and blotchy, chestnut-brown plumage. Rarely gives good views, except when discovered at daytime roost. At night, flies low on almost silent wings, whose rounded ends give it a distinctive appearance, even in silhouette.

Song and calls: Best-known for its repetitive, four-note song, often imitated by mischievous schoolboys or pranksters. The Tawny Owl's hooting can carry for up to a mile. Also gives a repeated, piercing call, 'kee-wick', with the accent on the second syllable.

Where and when: Found in rural and suburban gardens throughout Britain, even occasionally in town and city

adult

adult

centres, so long as there are trees for roosting and nesting. Tawny Owls are not found at all in Ireland. Present all year round.

Habits: Almost exclusively nocturnal, though may sometimes be seen roosting in a hole in a tree during the day. One of our most sedentary birds, rarely straying more than a mile or so from the heart of its territory.

Feeding: Feeds mainly on small rodents, including voles, mice

and rats. However, adaptable enough to take small birds and amphibians, especially when food resources are scarce due to harsh winter weather.

Breeding: After establishing their territory in late winter, Tawny Owls build their nest inside a hole or hollow in a tree. They lay between two and five eggs, which like those of most hole-nesting birds are white. Tawny Owls incubate for about four weeks, with the fluffy young fledging five weeks

later. Young may sometimes be seen outside a nest before they have fully fledged. Tawny Owls will readily take to suitable nestboxes.

SWIFT

Apus apus

The undisputed champion of all flying birds, the Swift is a familiar summer visitor to towns and cities throughout Britain and Ireland. Its piercing scream and coal-black plumage have earned it the folk-name 'devil bird'.

Identification features: 16–17 cm (6–7 in). With its all-dark plumage, long, pointed wings and short, stubby body, the Swift can be readily told apart from the unrelated House Martin and Swallow. Closer views reveal a pale throat, and paler edges to the wings. The tail is slightly forked.

Song and calls: A loud, piercing scream, often given by several birds at once as they fly overhead, especially in the early morning and at dusk.

Where and when: A summer visitor to Britain and Ireland, arriving in very late April or more usually in the first week of May. Swifts are a constant presence in our urban skies for

adult

adult

juvenile

the next couple of months, before heading back towards their African winter-quarters from late July or August onwards.

Habits: The only British bird which lives an almost exclusively aerial existence, only coming to land when breeding, and never landing on the ground. Because of this, Swifts are forced to avoid bad weather by flying away from it, sometimes for a considerable

distance, during which the young adopt a torpid state until their parents return.

Feeding: Swifts feed entirely on small flying insects, taken in flight.

Breeding: If the weather is fine, Swifts will start to breed almost as soon as they arrive here; while in cool, wet springs they may not begin until early June. They generally nest in high buildings, laying two or three white eggs, which they incubate

for between three and four weeks. The young fledge between five and eight weeks later, depending on the availability of insect food.

GREEN WOODPECKER

Picus viridis

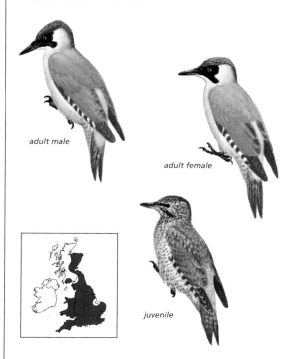

adult male

adult female

juvenile

Our largest woodpecker, roughly the size of a Collared Dove. Green Woodpeckers are shy birds, though if left undisturbed they will often visit garden lawns, where they feed on ants.

Identification features: 31–33 cm (12–13 in). A large, bulky woodpecker, easily told apart from our other native woodpeckers by size and plumage. Has yellowish-green upperparts, pale yellowish-buff underparts, a black face-mask and a red crown. In flight appears bulky, with a characteristic undulating motion. Juvenile is duller and more speckled, and lacks the adult's black mask.

Song and calls: A loud, far-carrying series of laughing notes, which has given the species the folk-name 'Yaffle'. Often said to call before rain, earning another folk-name: 'Rain bird'.

Where and when: Common and widespread in suitable habitat throughout England, Wales and southern Scotland north to Loch Ness. Like all woodpeckers, not found in Ireland. Will often visit gardens, especially those near woodland or parkland. Resident, present throughout the year.

Habits: A fairly shy and secretive bird, more often heard than seen. Prefers to feed on open grassy areas, though also seen perched on the sides of trees in typical woodpecker fashion. Rarely drums.

Feeding: Feeds mainly on ants, which it generally takes from the ground, using its specially adapted sticky tongue.

Breeding: In early spring Green Woodpeckers excavate a hole in the trunk or branch of a tree, where they lay between five and seven white eggs. They incubate for 17–19 days, and the young fledge 18–21 days later. One brood.

GREAT SPOTTED WOODPECKER

Dendrocopos major

Britain's most numerous and widespread woodpecker, the Great Spotted is also the bird responsible for the famous 'drumming' sound, made by rapidly beating its bill against the side of a hollow branch or tree trunk.

Identification features: 22–23 cm (9 in). A medium-sized woodpecker, about the size of a thrush. Male and female are boldly-patterned in black-and-white, with distinctive oval-shaped patches on the upperwing, and boldly barred flight feathers. Males have a small red patch on the back of the crown, and both sexes have a bright scarlet area on the lower belly. In the air, has distinctive undulating flight.

Song and calls: As well as the loud, distinctive drumming, both male and female also utter a loud, penetrating 'chip'.

Where and when: Found in suburban as well as rural areas throughout England and Wales, and in much of Scotland, though absent from much of the highlands and islands. Not found in Ireland. Resident, present throughout the year, though commoner in gardens during autumn and winter.

Habits: A brash, confident bird, generally the only woodpecker to regularly visit bird-feeders. Can be aggressive, often dominating smaller birds at peanut feeders and bird tables, sometimes even killing them.

Feeding: Mainly feeds on wood-boring insects, which it finds beneath the bark of trees, though adaptable enough to take nuts and fat from bird tables. Will also raid nestboxes and nest-holes for songbird chicks.

Breeding: Males start to drum early in the year, while excavating a suitable nest-hole in the branch or trunk of a tree. Lays between four and seven white eggs, which hatch 16 days later. The young fledge after 18–24 days. One brood.

adult male

adult female

juvenile

LESSER SPOTTED WOODPECKER

Dendrocopos minor

The smallest of our three breeding species of woodpecker, the Lesser Spotted is also by far the least common and hardest to see. More like a songbird than a woodpecker in its habits, it often skulks high in the foliage of a tree, staying frustratingly out of sight.

Identification features: 14–15 cm (6 in). Two-thirds the size of the Great Spotted, and shares its larger relative's pied plumage. Apart from size, there are some important plumage differences: Lesser Spotted lacks the oval patches on the wings, and has less distinct white barring. Overall, it appears less boldly-marked, and the underparts are pale with dark streaks, lacking the red belly of the Great Spotted. Male has a red patch on top of his crown, lacking in the female.

Song and calls: Drums quietly, though sometimes longer than Great Spotted. Call a high, repetitive but rather weak 'kee-

kee-kee-kee-kee-kee'.

Where and when: Found in small numbers in suitable wooded habitat throughout south-east England, and more widely scattered northwards to the Scottish border and westwards into Wales. Not found at all in Ireland. Resident, present throughout the year.

Habits: A shy and secretive bird, almost mouse-like in its habits. Creeps around trees in the manner of a Nuthatch or Treecreeper, rarely showing itself in the open. Will occasionally visit gardens, especially those with plenty of mature trees.

Feeding: Probes beneath the bark of trees for small insects and grubs.

Breeding: Excavates hole in tree, often in the very topmost branches. Lays between four and six white eggs, which hatch 11–14 days later. Young fledge after 18–21 days. One brood.

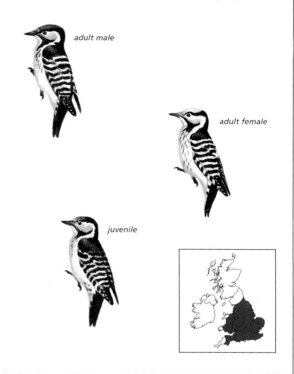

adult male

adult female

juvenile

KINGFISHER

Alcedo atthis

Our most brightly-coloured bird, the Kingfisher's blue and orange plumage is one of the most dazzling and memorable sights in the avian world. Living up to its name, the Kingfisher will make short work of fish in a garden pond.

Identification features: 16–17 cm (6–7 in). A much smaller bird than many people expect, barely larger than a sparrow. The combination of dazzling blue crown, tail and upperparts and deep rusty-orange underparts is unmistakable. Closer views reveal the huge, dagger-like bill, a white throat and white half-collar. In flight appears dazzling, especially when it catches the sun.

Song and calls: Gives a loud, strident, high-pitched whistle, often heard before the bird is seen.

Where and when: Although confined as a breeding bird to rivers, streams and lakes, Kingfishers often wander

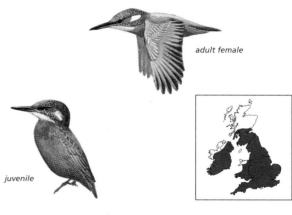

adult male

adult female

juvenile

surprising distances in search of food, especially during harsh winter weather. Fairly common and widespread throughout lowland parts of England and Wales; scarce in Scotland; thinly distributed in Ireland. Resident, present throughout the year, but tends to move towards coasts in winter.

Habits: Shy and retiring, its

presence often only given away by its call or a blinding flash of blue as it flies away. More likely to visit gardens early in the day, when there is less disturbance. If you have a pond, it should eventually attract one of these magnificent birds.

Feeding: Mainly feeds on small fish and aquatic invertebrates,

generally taken by plunge-diving beneath the surface of the water.

Breeding: Nests in a hole, usually in a sandbank or cliff-face overlooking water. Lays five to seven white eggs, which it incubates for 19–20 days. The young fledge three to four weeks later. Two, sometimes three, broods.

SWALLOW

Hirundo rustica

adult male

juvenile

One of our best-known summer visitors, the arrival of the first Swallow is the herald of spring throughout Britain and Europe. Languid and graceful, the Swallow is one of the bird world's most effective flying machines, making the long journey back and forth to southern Africa twice every year.
Identification features: 19–22 cm (7.5–9 in). More graceful, longer-winged and longer-tailed than the House Martin or Swift, and generally flies lower than either. Upperparts dark glossy blue; underparts off-white. Throat brick-red, bordered by blue breast-band. Long, deeply-forked tail, and swept-back wings. Juvenile duller, and has shorter tail than the adult.
Song and calls: Song a fast series of twittering notes, often uttered in flight. Call a high, lively-sounding 'chit'.

Where and when: A summer visitor, arriving back in April, and departing in September. Found throughout virtually the whole of Britain and Ireland, apart from urban areas, though less widespread in the extreme north.
Habits: Generally seen in flight, hawking low over the ground for insects. Also frequently perches on telegraph wires, especially just before migrating in late summer and autumn. May be seen in and around gardens, mainly in rural areas.
Feeding: Feeds exclusively on flying insects, caught in mid-air.
Breeding: Generally nests in buildings, such as barns (hence the alternative name 'Barn Swallow'), where it builds a cup-shaped nest from small particles of mud gathered nearby. Lays four or five whitish eggs with reddish-brown spots, which it incubates for 14–16 days. The young fledge three weeks later. Generally two, sometimes three, broods.

HOUSE MARTIN

Delichon urbica

One of the most familiar and welcome sights and sounds of summer, the House Martin has undergone a steady population decline in recent years, possibly due to droughts on its African wintering grounds. House Martins build a distinctive cup-shaped nest, made from mud, beneath the eaves of houses.
Identification features: 12.5 cm (5 in). Easily told apart from Swallow, Sand Martin and Swift by its bold white rump, dark blue upperparts and short, forked tail. Underparts plain snow-white, with greyish underwings.
Song and calls: Song a rapid series of twittering notes; also makes a short, sharp contact call: 'pritt'.
Where and when: A summer visitor, arriving back in April and early May, and departing south in August and September. Occasional stragglers may be

adult

adult

seen even later. Found more or less throughout Britain and Ireland, though scarce and localised in the extreme north and west.
Habits: Generally seen in flight or perched on telegraph wires. A noisy, sociable bird, always active: either feeding or nest-building. Once the young have hatched, spends most of the time going back and forth to the nest with food.
Feeding: Feeds almost exclusively on small insects, caught in mid-air.
Breeding: House Martins begin to build their semi-spherical nest almost as soon as they arrive back from Africa, using tiny balls of mud gathered from nearby ponds or puddles. Lays between three and five pale, whitish eggs, which it incubates for 14–16 days. Young fledge two to three weeks later. Two, occasionally three, broods.

GREY WAGTAIL
Motacilla cinerea

adult female summer

juvenile

adult male summer

adult male winter

More often associated with fast-flowing rivers and streams, the Grey Wagtail is an occasional visitor to gardens, mainly those in upland regions. Its elegant gait and delicate yellow, grey and black plumage distinguish it from its commoner relative, the Pied Wagtail.

Identification features: 18–19 cm (7–7.5 in). One of the most slender and long-tailed of all British birds, it can easily be told apart from Pied and Yellow Wagtails by the combination of slate-grey upperparts and lemon-yellow underparts, with varying amounts of white on the flanks and belly. The male in breeding plumage has a black throat, bordered by a white moustache. More likely to be seen outside the breeding season, when both male and female have a white throat and variable amounts of yellow beneath. In flight appears incredibly long and slender, with short wings and a bounding action.

Song and calls: A loud, strident, two-note 'chiz-zit', sharper and more metallic than the Pied Wagtail's call.

Where and when: Widely distributed throughout southern, western and northern Britain and most of Ireland, but surprisingly scattered and local in central and eastern England. Resident, present all year round, but more likely to visit gardens in autumn and winter.

Habits: Usually draws attention to itself by calling during flight, then landing on a rock, constantly wagging its long tail.

Feeding: Like other wagtails, feeds almost exclusively on insects, but will occasionally take small aquatic animals such as fish.

Breeding: Almost always breeds

by a river or stream, often building its nest in a crack in a wall or bridge. Lays between four and six buffish, spotted eggs, which it incubates for 11–14 days. The young fledge two weeks later. Usually two broods – sometimes three.

PIED WAGTAIL
Motacilla alba

adult female summer White

juvenile

adult male summer White

adult male winter White

adult male summer Pied

adult female summer Pied

adult female winter Pied

A familiar and attractive garden bird, this little black and white charmer is a frequent visitor to rural, suburban and urban gardens. Pied Wagtails often feed on paved areas or lawns, searching for tiny insects while constantly wagging their long tail.

Identification features: 18 cm (7 in). Its black and white plumage and characteristic horizontal gait make the Pied Wagtail unmistakable. Males have a black throat, crown and back, contrasting with their white face and underparts. The wings are streaked black and white, with two white wing-bars. Females are duller and greyer, while juveniles can look almost buffish. In flight shows long tail, short wings and characteristic 'bouncing' action.

Song and calls: A loud, characteristic 'chiz-zick', often given in flight. Song loud and twittering.

Where and when: Found virtually throughout Britain and Ireland, in a wide variety of habitats in lowland and upland areas. One of the few birds to be completely at home in our cities. White Wagtails are a scarce passage migrant to southern Britain.

Habits: An endearing little bird, as it constantly walks around a lawn or terrace in search of its food. Fairly sociable, especially in winter, when dozens of birds will gather together to roost against the cold.

Feeding: Feeds almost entirely on small insects, which it picks up off the ground or by digging into the surface of a lawn.

Breeding: Generally nests in cracks or holes in walls, building a cup-shaped nest lined with feathers or hair. Lays 5–6 pale eggs with fine spotting, which hatch 11–16 days later. The young fledge after 11–16 days. Usually raises two or three broods in a season.

WAXWING

Bombycilla garrulus

adult

juvenile

If you own a large garden near the east coast of Britain, with plenty of berry-bearing trees, then watch out for Waxwings! These rare, beautiful and much sought-after birds occasionally undergo 'irruptions', spreading west and south from their Scandinavian homes, and arriving in Britain during late autumn or early winter.
Identification features: 17–18 cm (6.5–7 in). Unmistakable! No other British bird has the

Waxwing's combination of plump shape, pinkish-beige plumage, soft, feathery crest and black, red and yellow wing-pattern. A close view also reveals the black throat and black 'highwayman's mask', and black and yellow tip to the tail. Roughly the size and shape of a Starling, which it can momentarily resemble in flight.
Song and calls: A soft, gentle trill, often given in unison by several birds in the flock.

Where and when: Waxwings are highly irregular in their movements; some winters bring tens of thousands to this country, others virtually none. They generally arrive from late October to December, though birds may spread westwards later in the winter, before leaving in March or April. Most likely to be seen in eastern England or Scotland.
Habits: Almost always seen in flocks, which descend on berry

bushes and gorge themselves on the ripe fruit, sometimes stripping the bush bare before moving on in search of new supplies. However, once they find a good food supply, they may stay in a single area for the whole of the winter.
Feeding: Mainly feeds on berries, especially large red ones. May also be seen catching flying insects, the normal diet during the breeding season.
Breeding: Does not breed in Britain or Ireland.

WREN

Troglodytes troglodytes

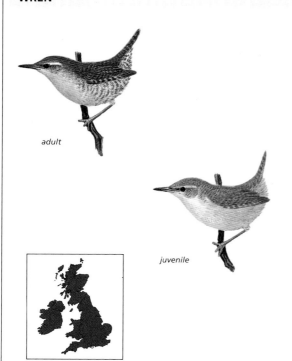

adult

juvenile

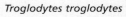

One of our smallest and most familiar birds, the Wren can nevertheless be surprisingly elusive, as it skulks around in dense undergrowth searching for food. Thanks to a long run of mild winters the Wren is now our commonest bird, with about ten million breeding pairs in Britain and Ireland.
Identification features: 9–10 cm (3.5–4 in). Tiny and pot-bellied, with a short, cocked tail. Generally appears brown, but closer views reveal delicate buff, grey and black markings. In flight, whirring wings and plump, rounded shape are diagnostic. Sexes alike.
Song and calls: Song one of the loudest of all songbirds: an extraordinary outburst of trills, ending with a flourish. Variety of calls, including a loud 'tic' and a churring rattle.
Where and when: Our most widespread bird, found virtually throughout Britain and Ireland, except in a very few

upland areas. Commonly found in gardens, though may be hard to see due to its skulking habits. Resident, present throughout the year.
Habits: Not a particularly shy bird, but tends to forage in dense undergrowth, only rarely appearing in the open. However, under some circumstances can be very confiding.
Feeding: Feeds mainly on tiny insects and other invertebrates, which it finds by foraging methodically amongst soil at the base of bushes and shrubs, or in the gaps between stones and rocks.
Breeding: Often breeds in gardens, building a well-concealed, dome-shaped nest in thick cover. Males may build several nests before the female chooses the final place to lay her five to eight, whitish eggs. The incubation period is 12–20 days, and the young fledge two to three weeks later. Nearly always has two broods.

DUNNOCK

Prunella modularis

fresh adult

worn adult

juvenile

A common, widespread yet easily-overlooked bird, the Dunnock's superficially drab appearance and retiring behaviour conceal an extraordinarily complex sex-life! Also known as the Hedge Sparrow, especially in rural areas, the Dunnock is in fact a member of the accentor family. **Identification features:** 14.5 cm (6 in). Although often considered to be just another 'little brown job', closer views reveal a delicately-marked and attractive bird, with purplish-grey head, neck and breast, and russet back and wings with black feather-centres. Legs pinkish-orange; bill thin and pointed, quite unlike that of a sparrow or a finch. **Song and calls:** A superficially nondescript but actually quite distinctive song: a rapid Wren-like warble which seems to have no obvious start or finish. Call a thin, piping 'tzeek'. **Where and when:** Found more or less throughout Britain and Ireland, though rare or absent in parts of north-west Scotland, and not found in Shetland. Resident, present throughout the year. **Habits:** Tends to skulk beneath bushes and shrubs, only rarely venturing out into the open. Creeps around in search of its food. **Feeding:** Feeds mainly on tiny invertebrates which it picks up from the ground. In winter, will also feed on small seeds, and if provided, mealworms. Often found beneath bird feeders, picking up spilt food. **Breeding:** Nests in dense undergrowth such as bramble bushes, building a neat, cup-shaped nest out of twigs and grasses, lined with feathers and hair. Lays between four and six sky-blue eggs, which hatch 12–13 days later. The young fledge after 11–12 days. Usually raises two, sometimes three, broods. Often polygamous, with 'spare' males muscling in on established pairs.

ROBIN

Erithacus rubecula

Britain's favourite garden bird, the Robin's attractive plumage and cheeky habits make it a welcome visitor to any garden, where it often becomes very tame. **Identification features:** The adult Robin is unmistakable, with its prominent orange-red face, throat and breast, beady black eye and plump shape. The crown, back, wings and tail are brown, and the belly greyish-white, with a grey line running from behind the eye to the flanks. Males and females are alike, and there is no difference between breeding and non-breeding plumages. Juvenile robins lack the red breast, and are generally spotted buff. **Song and calls:** The Robin's song is a beautiful, plaintive tune, sung throughout the year. Calls include a sharp 'tic', often repeated in rapid succession. **Where and when:** Found throughout Britain and Ireland,

adult

juvenile

in a wide range of gardens from city to country, though commonest in those near woodland. Present throughout the year, though in winter numbers are boosted by arrivals from the continent. **Habits:** Usually seen singing from a prominent perch, or hopping around on the ground in search of food. Robins often follow gardeners as they dig the soil, taking advantage of the worms and other invertebrates turned up by the spade. Generally solitary or in pairs, as males will not tolerate an intruder into their territory. **Feeding:** Takes a wide variety of invertebrate food, including earthworms. During autumn and winter diet changes to fruit and seeds, and will also come to feeders, especially during harsh weather. Enjoys mealworms. **Breeding:** An early nester, with males singing from January, and beginning to build nests from early March. Lays four to

six eggs, pale blue speckled with red, which it incubates for 13–15 days. Young are born blind, and fledge 12–14 days later. One or two broods.

REDSTART

Phoenicurus phoenicurus

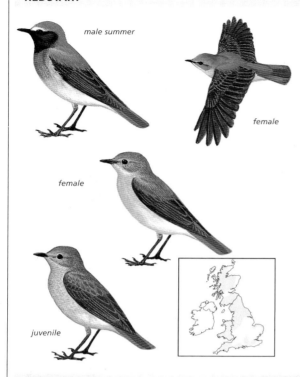

male summer

female

female

juvenile

Named after its colourful plumage ('start' means 'tail' in Old English), the Redstart is a summer visitor to Britain, found mainly in oak woodlands, and most common in upland areas of the north and west of the country.

Identification features: 13–14.5 cm (5–5.5 in). Given good views, the adult male Redstart is unmistakable, with brick-red breast and tail contrasting with a slate-grey back, black face and white forehead. Females are duller and paler, with mid-brown upperparts and buffish-orange underparts, though still showing the distinctive red in the tail.

Song and calls: The song is brief, high-pitched and fairly soft in tone, and may easily be missed amongst its louder cousins. Call a soft 'hoo-eet' together with a brief ticking. Males often sing from a prominent perch, usually at the top of a tree.

Where and when: A summer visitor to Britain, arriving in April and departing in September. Found mainly in mature oak woodlands in the north and west, particularly in Wales and Scotland, but also in the south-west and southern England. Very rare in Ireland. Only likely to be seen in large gardens with mature trees near suitable habitat.

Habits: For such a brightly coloured bird, the Redstart can be surprisingly elusive, though if seen near the nest it will usually give good views. Perches upright, and often flicks its tail to reveal the rusty-red colour.

Feeding: Eats insects and other invertebrates, taken from the ground, bark or foliage of trees.

Breeding: Nests in holes, either in a tree or stone building, or in a man-made nestbox. Lays five to seven light blue eggs, which it incubates for 11–15 days. The young fledge 12–15 days later. One, occasionally two, broods.

FIELDFARE

Turdus pilaris

adult

adult

juvenile

Although a few pairs breed in Britain, the Fieldfare is primarily a winter visitor to this country, arriving in large numbers from its breeding stronghold in Scandinavia. Like other thrushes, Fieldfares are particularly partial to berries, and are often seen in mixed feeding flocks with their smaller relative, the Redwing.

Identification features: 25–26 cm (10 in). A large, bulky thrush, only a shade smaller than its close relative the Mistle Thrush. At a distance appears greyish, but closer views reveal a striking and attractive bird, with a deep russet back, grey head, bright yellow bill and buffish-yellow underparts heavily marked with black. Has an undulating flight, revealing a grey rump contrasting with the black tail and russet wings and back. Sexes alike.

Song and calls: A harsh, repeated 'chack-chack-chack', generally given in flight.

Where and when: A common and widespread winter visitor to Britain and Ireland, though visits gardens rather less frequently than other thrushes, preferring to feed in fields and hedgerows. Harsh winter weather may force Fieldfares into gardens, particularly those in rural areas.

Habits: Much shyer than other members of its family, so may not spend long feeding in a single garden. Often perches on bushes where it can feed on berries, or comes onto open areas of lawn to find fruit.

Feeding: During autumn and winter feeds mainly on fruit and berries, either taken directly from the bush or from the ground.

Breeding: A recent colonist as a British breeding bird, confined to a few parts of the north and east of the country.

REDWING
Turdus iliacus

adult

juvenile

adult

Along with its larger relative the Fieldfare, the Redwing is a common winter visitor to most parts of Britain and Ireland, arriving in autumn from its breeding-grounds in Scandinavia and Iceland. In recent years small numbers have colonised northern Scotland as regular breeding birds.

Identification features: 21 cm (8 in). Easily distinguished from other thrushes by its smaller size, darker plumage, pale creamy eye-stripe and the reddish-orange patch on the flanks that gives the species its name. Throat and breast greyish-white, heavily streaked with brown; belly greyish-white; upperparts plain brown. In flight appears short-winged and short-tailed, reminiscent of a Starling, and may show rufous underwings. Sexes alike.

Song and calls: A thin, high-pitched 'tseep', usually uttered in flight.

Where and when: A common and widespread winter visitor throughout Britain and Ireland, often visiting gardens, especially in rural and suburban areas. Generally arrives from late October and November, and departs in March or early April. In harsh winter weather may migrate farther west, and disappear from eastern Britain.

Habits: Usually travels in flocks, often with other members of the thrush family. More likely to feed on the ground than Fieldfare, but like its larger cousin, also partial to stripping berries from bushes or trees. Commoner in gardens during colder weather, when food supplies may be scarce elsewhere.

Feeding: During autumn and winter feeds mainly on berries and windfall fruit. In the breeding season also takes insects.

Breeding: A recent colonist as a British breeding bird, virtually confined to a few parts of northern Scotland.

BLACKBIRD
Turdus merula

adult male
adult female
1st winter male
juvenile

This large and confident member of the thrush family is one of our most familiar and best-loved garden birds. The Blackbird is particularly prized for its beautiful, fluty song, which heralds the end of winter and the coming of spring.

Identification features: 24–25 cm (9–10 in). With his all-black plumage and bright yellow bill, the male Blackbird is unmistakable. Females are mid-brown, with some streaking on the underparts. Juveniles much streakier, almost resembling a thrush, though told apart by their more uniform plumage.

Song and calls: The male Blackbird's song is one of the quintessential sounds of the English garden. It is richly melodic, fluty, deep and slow, with deliberate pauses between each phrase. Blackbirds have a wide variety of calls, including a chattering alarm.

Where and when: Found throughout Britain and Ireland, apart from upland areas where it is replaced by the Ring Ousel. Common in most kinds of garden, though has recently suffered a population decline, so may be absent from former haunts. Resident, present throughout the year.

Habits: A brash, confident bird, often seen in the open as it feeds on lawns or sings from a prominent perch.

Feeding: During the breeding season feeds mainly on earthworms and other invertebrates, which it pulls from the soil or grass using its dagger-like bill. During autumn and winter will also eat fruit, especially berries and windfall apples.

Breeding: One of our earliest garden birds to begin breeding, it builds a cup-shaped nest lined with mud, in a bush or tree a metre or so above the ground. Lays between three and five pale greenish eggs, delicately spotted with reddish-brown, which it incubates for 12–15 days. The young fledge 12–15 days later, though are often fed by their parents after leaving the nest. May have up to five broods.

SONG THRUSH

Turdus philomelos

adult

adult

juvenile

Once one of our commonest garden birds, the Song Thrush has recently undergone a catastrophic decline, almost certainly due to modern farming methods reducing the availability of food. Some conservationists have predicted its eventual extinction as a British breeding bird, though hopefully a change in farming policy will reverse the decline.

Identification features: 23 cm (9 in). Distinguished from the Mistle Thrush by its smaller size, darker upperparts, and smaller, neater spotting on the underparts. Like all thrushes, has a distinctive upright appearance. Sexes alike.

Song and calls: The Song Thrush is aptly-named: its beautiful song is one of the best-loved of all our garden birds. Distinguished from Blackbird and Robin by its habit of repeating short phrases, often in groups of three. Call a thin, high-pitched 'tsip', given in flight.

Where and when: Despite its recent decline, still found throughout Britain and Ireland, though much less common than formerly. Resident, but autumn and winter see British birds heading south to be replaced by immigrants from Continental Europe.

Habits: Shyer than the Robin or Blackbird, the Song Thrush is nevertheless a familiar sight as it hops around the lawn in search of earthworms. In late winter often seen singing from a roof or tree, especially in the early evenings.

Feeding: Feeds mainly on snails, earthworms and other invertebrates. May be seen smashing snail shells on an 'anvil', in order to extract the contents.

Breeding: An early breeder, building a cup-shaped nest lined with mud, and laying between three and five sky-blue eggs spotted with black – described by the poet Gerard Manley Hopkins as 'little low heavens'. The eggs hatch after 12–14 days, and the young fledge 12–15 days later. Usually two, sometimes three, broods.

MISTLE THRUSH

Turdus viscivorus

The largest thrush found in Britain and Ireland, the Mistle Thrush is named for its fondness for berries, particularly that of the parasitic mistletoe plant. It is most often seen in gardens with large, mature trees, where it can build its nest and deliver its loud, fluty song.

Identification features: 27 cm (10.5 in). Not much smaller than a pigeon, the Mistle Thrush always appears larger and bulkier than its close relative the Song Thrush. Can also be told apart by its paler plumage, and denser spotting on the underparts. Upperparts greyish-brown, paler on wings; face palish, contrasting with large, dark eye; underparts yellowish-white, heavily spotted with black. In undulating flight, looks bulky, almost pigeon-like, and shows white outer tail-feathers. Sexes alike.

Song and calls: Song a rich, melodious series of phrases, less

adult

juvenile

adult

repetitive than Song Thrush and less rich than Blackbird. Main call given in flight: a distinctive harsh rattle.

Where and when: Found throughout Britain and Ireland, though rather less common in gardens than other members of its family, preferring areas of open parkland with large, well-scattered trees, or mixed woodland.

Habits: For such a large bird can be surprisingly shy and unobtrusive, though in spring the song usually betrays its presence. Will often perch on bushes to obtain berries, or hop across lawns.

Feeding: Feeds mainly on invertebrates such as earthworms, pulled from the ground. Also very partial to berries, and will defend a suitable bush against all-comers.

Breeding: Builds a large, cup-shaped nest in the fork of a tree, laying between three and five greenish-blue eggs, lightly speckled with brown. Incubates for 12–15 days, with the young fledging 12–16 days later. Two, sometimes three, broods.

GARDEN WARBLER

Sylvia borin

One of the least known and most unobtrusive of our common breeding warblers, the Garden Warbler is, despite its name, not a very common garden visitor. Shy, nondescript and thinly distributed, it is very easily overlooked.

adult

juvenile

Identification features: 14 cm (5.5 in). A fairly large warbler, with few identification features. Close views reveal a greyish-brown back, pale grey underparts, and an unmarked head and face with a prominent dark eye. Best distinguished by song, though even this can be difficult! Sexes alike.

Song and calls: Song a rapid warbling series of notes, often very similar to that of its close relative the Blackcap, but faster and with less variety, lacking the latter's rich, fluty tone.

Where and when: A summer visitor to Britain, widespread but thinly scattered across most of England, Wales and southern Scotland, with a few birds north to Orkney. Also found in a few parts of Ireland. Arrives in early or mid-May, and leaves by August.

Habits: A shy, skulking bird, usually discovered by its song, and only seen after much persistence on the part of the observer. Prefers dense undergrowth, such as small copses. Generally only found in rural gardens with lots of suitable cover.

Feeding: Feeds mainly by gleaning for tiny insects and other invertebrates in dense foliage.

Breeding: After returning from its African winter-quarters, Garden Warblers quickly set up a territory and begin breeding. Males may build several nests in thick cover, often close to the ground, with the female selecting the most suitable. Lays four or five pale eggs, lightly spotted with brown, which hatch after 10–12 days. Young fledge after just 9–12 days. One, sometimes two, broods.

BLACKCAP

Sylvia atricapilla

A large, grey warbler with the distinctive plumage feature giving the bird its name: the male's crown is black, while the female's is chestnut-brown. In recent years has become a much more regular garden visitor, thanks to a boom in the breeding population and the start of regular wintering by birds from central Europe.

adult male

adult female

juvenile

Identification features: 14 cm (5.5 in). A large warbler, less shy than other members of its family, and easy to identify thanks to its distinctive cap. This contrasts with the rest of the plumage, which is rather plain grey – darker above than below.

Song and calls: Often located by its distinctive song: obviously warbler-like in character, but with sweet, fluty notes reminiscent of a Blackbird or even Nightingale in character. Also gives a hard, pebble-like 'tac'.

Where and when: Formerly purely a summer visitor to Britain and Ireland, returning in late March or April and departing in August and September. However, during the last few decades birds from Germany and Austria have begun to migrate to Britain, spending the winter here in ever-growing numbers. During the breeding season commonest in England, Wales and southern Scotland, and rarer farther north; in winter commonest in the south and east of Britain. Scattered but widespread in Ireland.

Habits: As warblers go, fairly confident and easy to see, though may still hide in dense foliage, or high in the canopy of trees. During the autumn and winter often visits gardens to feed.

Feeding: During the breeding season feeds almost exclusively on small insects, gleaned from bushes and trees. However, autumn and winter visitors feed mainly on fruit.

Breeding: An early summer migrant, often starting to breed at the beginning of April. Builds a nest in low, thick foliage, and lays between four and six pale eggs, finely spotted with brown, which hatch 10–12 days later. Young fledge after 10–13 days. One or two broods.

WILLOW WARBLER

Phylloscopus trochilus

adult spring

adult autumn

juvenile

Although not as well-known as the Swift or Swallow, the Willow Warbler is in fact our commonest summer migrant, with more than three million breeding pairs in Britain and Ireland. Its distinctive song is one of the quintessential sounds of a woodland in spring or summer.

Identification features: 11.5 cm (4.5 in). A small, nondescript, greenish-coloured warbler, best told apart from its close relative the Chiffchaff by its distinctive silvery song. Given close views,

its brighter plumage, pale legs and more prominent pale eye-stripe are also good distinguishing features. Juvenile can appear brighter green, with yellowish underparts. Sexes alike.

Song and calls: Delightful song: a plaintive, melodic series of notes, descending the scale with a shudder. Call a quiet 'hoo-eet', quite similar to Chaffinch.

Where and when: A summer visitor, found virtually throughout Britain and Ireland apart from the high mountain-

tops and Shetland. Particularly common in areas of birch woodland, but also a frequent visitor to gardens in rural areas, or those near woodland or heath.

Habits: Often sings from a very prominent perch, though because of its small size may still be hard to spot. Otherwise typically warbler-like in its habits, gleaning insect food while hopping about in bushes and trees.

Feeding: Feeds almost exclusively on insects taken by flycatching or gleaning; will also eat fruit, especially in late summer.

Breeding: Builds a small, domed nest in dense cover, which it lines with feathers, usually on or very near the ground. Lays between four and eight white eggs, lightly speckled reddish-brown, which hatch 12–14 days later. The young fledge after 11–15 days. One, sometimes two, broods.

CHIFFCHAFF

Phylloscopus collybita

adult spring

adult autumn

juvenile

The Chiffchaff's well-known and distinctive song is one of the earliest signs that spring is just around the corner. It is also by far the easiest way to distinguish this species from its almost identical relative, the Willow Warbler. Once purely a summer migrant to Britain and Ireland, Chiffchaffs now regularly overwinter here too.

Identification features: 11 cm (4–4.5 in). A small, nondescript warbler, with a brownish-green plumage and few distinguishing

marks. Usually browner and less well-marked than Willow Warbler, with darker legs and a shorter, pale stripe above the eye. Best identified by its distinctive song. Sexes alike.

Song and calls: Uniquely distinctive song, repeating a series of two sounds: 'chiff-chaff-chiff-chaff-chiff-chaff'. Also utters a low, plaintive 'whee-eet'.

Where and when: A common summer visitor to Britain and Ireland, though rare or

localised in northern Scotland and absent from Shetland. Arrives earlier than most migrants, often in March, and most leave in September. Wintering birds are mainly found in the south and west, generally near water.

Habits: Usually seen flitting around in bushes or trees, searching for tiny morsels of food amongst the twigs and branches. Often sings from an obvious perch.

Feeding: During the breeding season feeds almost exclusively on insects, which it gleans amongst the foliage. In winter has adapted to feeding on fruit and even peanuts from artificial feeders.

Breeding: Builds a well-concealed nest on the ground or low in cover, laying between four and seven whitish eggs with dark spots. The young hatch after 13–15 days and fledge 12–15 days later. One, occasionally two, broods.

GOLDCREST

Regulus regulus

Our smallest and lightest bird, measuring nine centimetres long, and weighing just five grams – the same as a 20p piece! Often associated with conifers, the Goldcrest may be glimpsed as it flits from twig to twig, or given away by its thin, high-pitched call.

Identification features: 9 cm (3.5 in). A tiny, jewel-like bird, superficially resembling a small warbler, but distinguished by the head-pattern which gives the species its name. Yellowish-green upperparts; dark wings edged with white; pale underparts. Large, beady eye; tiny black bill. Adult male and female have broad golden-yellow crown-stripe, bordered with black. Males sometimes show orange centre to crown. Juveniles lack the crown-stripe and may be confused with Chiffchaff or Willow Warbler, though small size and plump shape distinctive.

Song and calls: Song a rhythmic, high-pitched, three-note phrase, with a distinctive cyclical quality. Call a very high-pitched 'see-see-see', too high for some human ears.

Where and when: Widespread throughout most parts of Britain and Ireland, particularly Scotland and southern Ireland. Often associated with conifers, preferring gardens with trees such as holly or yew. More likely to visit gardens during autumn and winter.

Habits: Can be very hard to see, though patient listening and looking will generally reveal its presence. In winter, often associates with mixed flocks of tits.

Feeding: Feeds almost exclusively on tiny insects, obtained by picking off leaves and twigs, or by 'hover-gleaning' by the end of a branch.

Breeding: Mostly nests in conifers, building a tiny nest from moss, often hanging on the tip of a twig. Lays between seven and twelve tiny, pale eggs, finely spotted buff, which it incubates for 16 days. The young fledge 19 days later. A second clutch may be laid almost immediately, even before the first brood have fledged.

adult male

adult female

juvenile

SPOTTED FLYCATCHER

Muscicapa striata

This delightful little bird is well-named, as it feeds by launching itself off a twig or branch to catch insects in flight. The Spotted Flycatcher is one of our latest summer visitors to arrive back from its African winter-quarters, with most returning towards the end of May.

Identification features: 14 cm (5.5 in). At first sight, may appear to be just another 'little brown job'. But take a closer look, and you'll see a slim, greyish-buff bird with a beady eye, thin bill and delicate streaking on the crown and breast. Has a distinctive, 'upright' posture, and in flight shows very long wings. Sexes alike.

Song and calls: High-pitched, rather short series of squeaky notes, usually delivered from a perch on a twig or branch.

Where and when: Found in small numbers more or less throughout Britain and Ireland, though rare in the extreme north and west of Scotland, and absent from Shetland. Prefers larger gardens, with plenty of trees and walls in which to nest. Summer visitor, returning from the middle of May and leaving by September.

Habits: Best-known for the feeding method which gives the family its name: leaping into thin air to grab an unsuspecting insect, before returning to its perch.

Feeding: Almost entirely on small flying insects which it catches in flight, or gleans from leaves of trees.

Breeding: Builds a shallow nest in a hole or crevice in a wall. Lays four to six buffish or greenish-blue eggs with red speckles. Incubates for 12–14 days, and young fledge about two weeks later. Unseasonally wet weather and the resulting shortage of food, may mean that the chicks starve. However, in warm, dry summers many pairs manage a second, smaller clutch, the young of which may be fed by the first brood.

adult

juvenile

LONG-TAILED TIT

Aegithalos caudatus

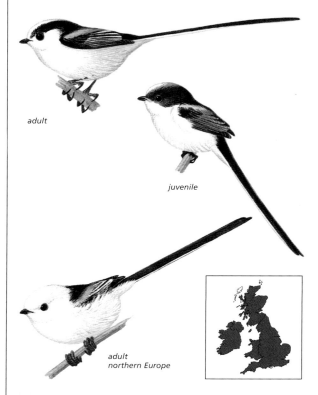

adult

juvenile

*adult
northern Europe*

With its small size, long tail and distinctive plumage, the Long-tailed Tit is one of our most endearing garden birds. Like other members of the tit family, if often travels in flocks, which signal their arrival by uttering noisy, twittering contact calls.

Identification features: 12–14 cm (5–5.5 in). The plump, fluffy body, long tail and combination of black, cream and pink plumage mean that given good views, the Long-tailed Tit is unmistakable. The head is creamy-white, with a thick black stripe running above the eye to the dark nape. Upperparts are buffish-pink, with black wings showing pale edges to the feathers. Underparts dirty cream, with pinkish wash on the belly and flanks.

Song and calls: Utters a wide range of thin, high-pitched sounds, often repeated excitedly in order to keep in touch with the rest of the flock.

Where and when: Found throughout most of Britain, though rare in northern Scotland and absent from the western and northern isles. Widely but thinly distributed in Ireland. Resident, present throughout the year, though much commoner in gardens during the autumn and winter.

Habits: Usually travels in noisy, excitable flocks, which give away their presence by continually calling while flitting from twig to twig in search of food. May allow very close approach, as often seem almost oblivious to human presence.

Feeding: Feeds mainly on tiny insects and spiders, obtained by gleaning from leaves, twigs and branches.

Breeding: A fairly early breeder, often beginning in March. Builds a unique barrel-shaped nest from tiny feathers, which it glues together with thread from spiders' webs and covers with lichen in order to provide camouflage. Lays between seven and twelve tiny white eggs, which it incubates for 13–17 days. The young fledge 15–16 days later. One brood.

MARSH TIT

Parus palustris

Unlike its familiar relatives the Blue and Great Tits, the Marsh Tit is not a particularly common garden visitor, although it may still be seen coming to feeders, especially in gardens near woodland. Its rather dull plumage may also mean that it is sometimes overlooked.

Identification features: 11.5 cm (4.5 in). Like all tits, the Marsh Tit is small, plump and active. It can be told apart from all but the Willow Tit by its black cap and bib, pale cheeks, and uniformly brown upperparts. Underparts are buffish. May be confused with superficially similar Coal Tit, but less colourful, and lacks the distinctive white patch on the back of the nape. The very similar Willow Tit is now a very rare breeding bird, and unlikely to be seen in most gardens. Sexes alike.

Song and calls: Song a repetitive, monotonous series of monosyllabic notes. Call a sharp 'pit-choo'.

Where and when: Virtually confined as a British breeding bird to England and Wales, though a few breed in the extreme south-east of Scotland. Not found at all in Ireland. Resident, present throughout the year, though more likely to visit gardens in winter.

Habits: Shyer than Blue and Great Tits, but will still visit bird tables and feeders. However, it is less dominant than the commoner species, often staying for only a moment or two before flying off again. Otherwise may be seen in trees or bushes.

Feeding: During the breeding season feeds mainly on insects. In autumn and winter will also take berries, or feed on seeds and peanuts from artificial feeders.

Breeding: A hole-nester, usually in a natural hole or crevice in a rotten tree. Lays between seven and eleven white eggs, with a few reddish spots, which hatch after 13–15 days. Young fledge 17–21 days later.

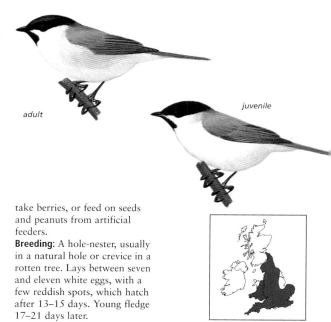

adult

juvenile

COAL TIT

Parus ater

A small, active, acrobatic little bird, the Coal Tit is one of our most endearing of all garden visitors. Though not so brightly-coloured as Blue and Great Tits, they are nevertheless highly attractive. Though they breed mainly in coniferous forests and plantations, they often visit gardens, especially in winter.

Identification features: 11.5 cm (4.5 in). Usually appears smaller and slimmer than other members of its family. Combination of brownish plumage, black cap and throat, white cheeks and white nape (back of neck) are distinctive. Wings dark with two obvious wingbars, quite unlike the plain-winged Marsh Tit. Sexes alike.

Song and calls: Song a rhythmic, repetitive series of notes, recalling a weaker version of Great Tit. Call thin and very high-pitched, similar to Goldcrest.

adult

juvenile

Where and when: Found more or less throughout Britain and Ireland, apart from treeless areas such as the East Anglian fens, and Orkney and Shetland. Resident, present throughout the year, but more likely to visit gardens during autumn and winter.

Habits: A highly active, acrobatic bird, often hanging upside down in order to get food. Easily adapts to taking food from artificial feeders. Often appears in small flocks, with other tit species.

Feeding: During the breeding season feeds mainly on insects and small spiders, obtained by gleaning pine needles. Will also take nuts from feeders.

Breeding: Builds a cup-shaped nest out of moss, inside the cavity of a rotten tree stump or branch, or amongst tree-roots, usually very close to the ground. Lays eight or nine white eggs, with a few brownish-red spots, which it incubates for 13–18 days. Young fledge 16–22 days later. One, sometimes two, broods.

BLUE TIT

Parus caeruleus

Our commonest species of tit, and undoubtedly one of the best-known and best-loved of all our garden birds. Blue Tits are highly adaptable, able to live alongside human beings and learn new habits very quickly.

Identification features: 11.5 cm (4.5 in). Easily distinguished from the Great Tit by its smaller size, blue crown and back, and far less black in the plumage. Blue crown and nape contrast with white cheeks and thin black stripe through the eye and around the neck and throat. Underparts greenish-yellow, with a narrow dark stripe down the belly. Back olive-green; wings bluish with a white wingbar; tail blue. Sexes more or less alike: the male has a slightly broader black necklace than the female. Juvenile much duller, with yellow wash on face and greenish cap.

Song and calls: Wide variety of

adult

juvenile

calls, including trills, scolding chatter and high-pitched 'tsee-tsee-tsee'.

Where and when: Found throughout most of Britain and Ireland, absent only from Orkney, Shetland and parts of north and west Scotland. Resident, found in gardens throughout the year, though commoner in winter.

Habits: A noisy, sociable bird, often squabbling amongst themselves or with other garden species. Able to learn new

habits, including the ability to peck open milk-bottle tops to obtain the cream inside!

Feeding: During the breeding season feeds mainly on insects and small spiders. In autumn and winter relies much more on seeds and peanuts from artificial feeders.

Breeding: A hole-nester, using either a natural cavity in a tree, or where available, an artificial nestbox. Lines the cavity with moss, grass and feathers, then lays between seven and sixteen

white eggs, with a few spots. The incubation period lasts for 13–16 days, and the young fledge between 16 and 22 days later. One brood.

GREAT TIT

Parus major

adult male

juvenile

By far the largest member of the tit family found in Britain or Ireland, the Great Tit is bold, bright and brash, easily dominating its smaller cousins at bird tables and feeders. It is also highly adaptable, readily taking to artificial nestboxes.

Identification features: 13.5–14.5 cm (5.5–6 in). Easily distinguished from all other tits by its larger size and bold black and yellow plumage. Crown, neck and throat jet-black, contrasting with bright white cheeks. Back greenish; wings bluish-black with white edges and a bold white wingbar. Underparts bright lemon-yellow, bisected by a bold black stripe from the throat to the belly. Sexes more or less alike: the male is brighter with a thicker black belly stripe.

Song and calls: Song a loud, repetitive two-note utterance, often transcribed as 'tea-cher, tea-cher', with the accent on the second syllable. Also gives a

wide variety of other calls which may confuse the experienced birder as well as the novice!

Where and when: Found throughout most of Britain and Ireland, apart from most of the Western Isles and Orkney and Shetland. Resident, present in gardens throughout the year, though commoner in autumn and winter.

Habits: A brash, confident bird, rarely afraid to take advantage of the free food supply offered by bird tables and other

artificial feeders. In spring, males sing from a prominent perch.

Feeding: During the breeding season, prefers large caterpillars, but at other times of year will generally take peanuts and seeds.

Breeding: A hole-nester, either using a hole in a tree or a nestbox. Lays between five and eleven white eggs with reddish spots, which it incubates for 11–15 days. The young fledge three weeks later. One, sometimes two, broods.

NUTHATCH

Sitta europaea

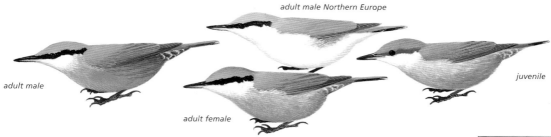

adult male Northern Europe

adult male

adult female

juvenile

The only British bird able to climb vertically down the trunk of a tree, the Nuthatch is one of our best-adapted woodland species. In recent years it has become an increasingly frequent visitor to gardens, where it has learned to take nuts from artificial feeders.

Identification features: 14 cm (5.5 in). A handsome and distinctive bird, with blue-grey cap and upperparts, orange-buff underparts and a bold black stripe through the eye, giving the appearance of a

'highwayman's mask'. Throat paler than rest of underparts, while belly may be darker, almost rusty brown. Shape also very distinctive: large, powerful beak, pot belly and short, stubby tail. Sexes alike.

Song and calls: A loud and far-carrying 'pee-uu... pee-uu', with a distinctive echoic quality.

Where and when: Found throughout wooded areas of England and Wales, with a few birds breeding in south-east Scotland. Not found at all in Ireland. Resident, present

throughout the year, though more likely to visit gardens in winter. Fairly sedentary.

Habits: As already mentioned, the only bird which can climb down, as well as up, a tree-trunk. Highly acrobatic. Rarely flies, except to move from tree to tree.

Feeding: During the breeding season feeds mainly on insects, but in autumn and winter will regularly take peanuts from feeders. Also has habit of hoarding nuts as an insurance against harsh winter weather.

Breeding: A hole-nester, using natural holes or crevices in mature trees. Lays between six and eight white eggs with reddish spots, which hatch between 13 and 18 days later. Young fledge after 23–24 days. One brood.

TREECREEPER

Certhia familiaris

The aptly-named Treecreeper spends most of its time creeping around the branches and trunks of trees, constantly searching for tiny insects to eat. Unlike the Nuthatch, however, Treecreepers can only climb up, not down!

Identification features: 12.5 cm (5 in). A small, slender, mouse-like bird with streaked greyish-brown upperparts, paler underparts and a long, decurved bill which it uses to probe beneath the bark of trees for insects. Closer views reveal a pale stripe above the eye, and buffish shading around the lower part of the belly. Sexes alike.

Song and calls: Song a thin, high-pitched trill, like a weaker version of the Wren's song. Call a thin 'tseee', similar to Goldcrest.

Where and when: Found in suitable wooded habitat throughout Britain, apart from the Western Isles, Orkney and

adult

juvenile

Shetland. Also thinly distributed throughout Ireland. Resident, present throughout the year. Very sedentary, and so vulnerable to cold spells in winter.

Habits: Unobtrusive but fairly confiding, usually seen crawling up a tree trunk or along a branch before taking a short, weak flight to the next tree. Easily overlooked. Often looks superficially like a mouse rather than a bird.

Feeding: Feeds exclusively on

tiny insects and other invertebrates obtained by probing beneath the bark with its long, slender bill.

Breeding: Builds a nest in a tiny crack or crevice in the bark of a tree, where it lays five or six white eggs with brownish spots, which it incubates for 13–15 days. Young fledge 14–16 days later. One, often two, broods. Sometimes uses specially-designed nestboxes fixed beneath the underside of a branch.

JAY

Garrulus glandarius

Like the other members of the crow family, Jays are adaptable and highly intelligent birds, always on the lookout for food. They are also fearsome predators, stealing eggs or chicks from nests whenever the opportunity presents itself.

Identification features: 34 cm (13 in). With their distinctive pinkish-brown plumage, striking head-pattern and bright blue wing-edges, Jays are quite different from other members of their family. Upperparts may appear brown or pink, depending on the light. Underparts are paler, shading to white on the lower belly. Head shows a strong, broad black moustache, and a streaked black and white crown. Wings and tail are black, with a white patch on the centre of the wing, and a blue edge to the forewing. Sexes alike. In flight, shows white wing-patches and white rump.

Song and calls: Varied repertoire

adult

juvenile

adult

of harsh, screeching calls.

Where and when: Found throughout England and Wales, though much commoner in south-east England and the Welsh borders than elsewhere. Also found in lowland areas of southern and central Scotland. Distinctive race found in parts of Ireland. Resident, though in autumn and winter numbers may be augmented by the arrival of birds from Continental Europe.

Habits: For such a large, fierce and colourful bird, the Jay can be surprisingly shy and unobtrusive. However, the

patient observer may be rewarded with close views of this splendid bird.

Feeding: Like other crows, largely omnivorous, feeding on insects, seeds, nuts and the eggs and chicks of songbirds. Also has a strong preference for acorns, which it may hoard for later use.

Breeding: Builds a cup of twigs, usually in the fork of a tree, where it lays between five and eight pale olive eggs, speckled with brown. Jays incubate for 16–17 days, and the young fledge 19–23 days later. One brood.

MAGPIE

Pica pica

adult

juvenile

adult

This handsome bird is regarded by many people as a bloodthirsty villain, responsible for the recent decline in numbers of our garden birds. In fact although Magpies do sometimes take eggs and chicks, their effect on songbird populations has been proved to be minimal.

Identification features: 44–48 cm (17–19 in). With its long tail and black and white plumage, the Magpie is surely unmistakable. Head, back, throat and upper breast are black; lower breast and belly white. Wings black with a bluish-green sheen and large oval white patches; tail greenish-black. Powerful black bill. Juveniles lack the adults' long tail. Sexes alike.

Song and calls: A harsh, rattling call, like a slow-firing machine gun.

Where and when: Common and widespread throughout England and Wales, especially in the south and west, but in Scotland largely confined to the south-west and north-east. Magpies are especially common in Ireland, where they reach some of their highest densities in the world. Resident, present throughout the year.

Habits: A noisy, sociable bird, whose flocking habits are celebrated in rhyme ('One for sorrow, two for joy...'). Has an ambiguous and wary relationship with humans, and will often flee if approached too closely.

Feeding: Largely omnivorous, taking plant and animal food, or feeding on nuts and kitchen scraps. Also takes eggs and chicks during the breeding season.

Breeding: Builds a loose, untidy nest from sticks, high in a bush or tree. Lays between five and eight pale greenish-blue eggs, with reddish-brown blotches, which hatch after 17–18 days. Young fledge 22–28 days later. One brood.

JACKDAW

Corvus monedula

adult

juvenile

adult

The smallest member of the crow family found in Britain, the Jackdaw is a quintessentially rural bird, found in villages and farming areas throughout the country. It is sociable and intelligent, making it one of the most fascinating birds to watch.

Identification features: 33 cm (13 in). Smaller than the Rook or Carrion Crow, and easily distinguished by the pale greyish patch on the back and sides of its neck. The rest of the plumage is glossy blue-black, with a noticeable pale eye. Bill short and black. In flight looks short-winged and compact, though best identified by its characteristic call. Sexes alike.

Song and calls: An unmistakable, harsh 'chak', which gives the Jackdaw its name.

Where and when: Common and widespread throughout rural England, Wales, southern and eastern Scotland. Patchily distributed in northern and western Scotland, and Orkney (but not Shetland). Very common and widespread in Ireland. Resident, present throughout the year.

Habits: Gregarious and sociable, often seen in large, noisy, quarrelsome flocks. May perch on roofs before venturing into a garden for food.

Feeding: Feeds on a wide range of plant and animal food, and will also take a variety of food provided by humans.

Breeding: A colonial breeder, building its nest in a hole or crevice in brick or stone, or from sticks in a tree. Lays

between four and six pale bluish-green eggs, with dark blotches, which hatch 17–18 days later. Young fledge after four or five weeks. One brood.

ROOK

Corvus frugilegus

Like its smaller cousin the Jackdaw, the Rook is one of the typical birds of the British and Irish countryside. Known for their very public nesting habits, Rooks are only an occasional visitor to gardens, mainly in rural areas. They are also widely associated with folklore, especially weather forecasting!

Identification features: 47 cm (18.5 in). A large, mainly black bird, told apart from Carrion Crow by its distinctive, pointed, greyish-white bill and face; smaller, more angular head; and thinner, more rakish appearance. Close-up, or in certain lights, the plumage may appear almost navy-blue or even purple. In flight appears more slender and narrower-winged than Carrion Crow, with a more buoyant action. Sexes alike.

Song and calls: A wide range of deep, harsh, grating calls, including the well-known 'caw'.

Where and when: Widely though sometimes thinly distributed throughout rural England, Wales and southern and eastern Scotland, as far north as Orkney. Common and widespread throughout Ireland. Resident, present throughout the year.

Habits: One of the most sociable of all birds, almost always seen in flocks. Often gather to feed in fields, with other members of the crow family such as Jackdaws.

Feeding: Feeds on a wide variety of plant and animal food, including acorns, earthworms and grain.

Breeding: Breeds in colonies, in large rookeries, building an untidy nest from sticks in the tops of trees. Lays between three and six pale bluish eggs, blotched with brown, which hatch 16–18 days later. Young fledge after 29–33 days. One brood.

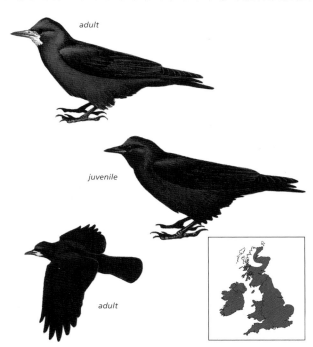

adult

juvenile

adult

CARRION, HOODED CROW

Corvus corone

For people living in towns and cities throughout Britain, the Carrion Crow is the typical large black bird: noisy, obvious and faintly disturbing, like something out of Hitchcock's *The Birds*. Although quite different in appearance, the Hooded Crow is usually considered to be a well-marked race of the same species, though some ornithologists now consider the two to be separate species.

Identification features: 47 cm (18.5 in). Carrion Crow is the only completely black bird found in Britain. Its combination of large size and all-black bill distinguish it from the Rook and Jackdaw. Hooded Crow has a black head, neck and bib, black wings and tail, which contrast with its grey back and underparts. Sexes alike. Occasionally hybrids appear in parts of Scotland, showing intermediate characteristics between the two races.

juvenile Hooded

juvenile Carrion

adult Carrion

adult Hooded

adult Hybrid

adult Carrion

adult Hooded

Song and calls: Both Carrion and Hooded Crows have an identical call: a harsh, strident 'caw'.

Where and when: Carrion Crow is widely distributed throughout England, Wales, and most of Scotland, apart from the extreme north and west. A few birds also breed in north-east Ireland. The Hooded Crow replaces the Carrion Crow in north and west Scotland, the Isle of Man and Ireland.

Habits: Carrion Crows regularly visit gardens in search of food, sometimes in large flocks. In contrast, Hooded Crows are mainly rural birds, though may visit gardens in these areas. Both are dominant over most other species.

Feeding: Omnivorous, taking seeds, fruit, insects, and the eggs and chicks of smaller birds. Will also readily take kitchen scraps where available.

Breeding: Builds a large, loose nest from twigs and sticks, usually in a tree, but occasionally on cliff-faces or buildings. Lays between four and six pale bluish-green eggs, blotched with reddish-brown, which it incubates for 17–21 days. The young fledge four to five weeks later. One brood.

STARLING

Sturnus vulgaris

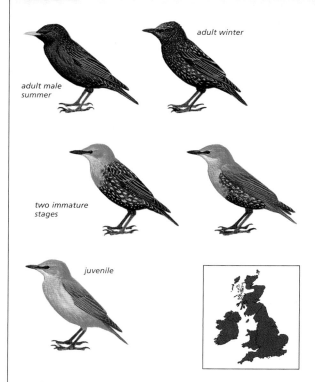

adult winter

adult male summer

two immature stages

juvenile

One of our most familiar yet easily-overlooked garden birds, the Starling has an undeserved reputation for vulgarity and boorish behaviour. In fact it is an attractive and fascinating bird, which in recent years has begun to decline for reasons as yet unknown.

Identification features: 21 cm (8 in). Adult Starlings are quite distinctive: a dark bird the size of a small thrush, with a sharp yellow bill and glossy blue-black plumage tinged with green, and covered in fine pale spots. In breeding plumage appears brighter and less spotty, with a glossy head and neck. Juvenile dull brown, with dark grey bill. Sexes very similar, though the male has a bluish base to the bill.

Song and calls: Starlings are brilliant mimics, able to imitate a huge range of natural and artificial sounds, including other birds as well as telephones and burglar alarms! Also has variety of whistling calls.

Where and when: Common and widespread throughout virtually the whole of Britain and Ireland, only absent from upland areas of the Scottish Highlands. Northern and Western Isles have distinctive, brighter-plumaged race. Resident, present throughout the year.

Habits: A gregarious and sociable bird, generally seen in large flocks. Often visits gardens with open lawns to feed, and will also come to artificial feeders and bird tables.

Feeding: Feeds on a wide variety of natural and artificial food, but especially partial to invertebrates obtained by digging into short grass with their long, pointed bill.

Breeding: Nests in holes and crevices, filled with grass or other plant matter. Lays between four and seven pale blue eggs, which hatch after 12–15 days. Young fledge about three weeks later. One or two broods.

HOUSE SPARROW

Passer domesticus

We once took them for granted, but House Sparrows are becoming increasingly scarce in many parts of the country. This decline is due to modern farming methods, which have reduced the amount of food available for this familiar bird.

Identification features: 15 cm (6 in). Everyone knows the House Sparrow: the male with his smart black bib, grey crown and creamy white cheeks; and the female – surely the ultimate 'little brown job'! In fact both male and female have a delicately marked plumage: the male's upperparts intermingle black, buff, chestnut and grey, with a dull wingbar, while the female has a distinctive creamy-buff streak through the eye. Both sexes have greyish-brown underparts.

Song and calls: Song a random collection of cheeping and chirping notes. Gives a variety of calls, including the classic 'chirrup'.

Where and when: Found throughout lowland Britain and Ireland, including most offshore islands; only absent from the Scottish Highlands. However, recently undergoing a dramatic decline, especially in gardens. Resident, present throughout the year.

Habits: A noisy, gregarious bird, usually seen in small, quarrelsome groups. Very used to humans, and one of the boldest species when it comes to taking food.

Feeding: Natural diet includes insects during the breeding season, and seeds and grain during autumn and winter, but will also take advantage of food provided by humans, especially peanuts.

Breeding: As its name suggests, generally breeds close to human habitation, often nesting under the eaves of houses. Lays between three and six pale eggs speckled with brown and grey, which hatch after 11–14 days. The young fledge 14–19 days later. Up to three, occasionally four, broods.

adult male hybrid with Tree Sparrow

adult male winter

juvenile

adult male summer

adult female

TREE SPARROW

Passer montanus

adult

juvenile

Once widespread and fairly common, in recent years the Tree Sparrow population has undergone a more rapid decline than any other British breeding species. Should this continue, this charming little bird may eventually disappear from our countryside.

Identification features: 14 cm (5.5 in). Although superficially similar to its more familiar relative, the Tree Sparrow is in fact a quite distinctive looking bird. Both male and female have a bright chestnut-brown cap, which contrasts with the white collar and a small black spot just behind the eye. The upperparts are similar to the male House Sparrow, though rather cleaner and brighter, while the underparts are grey.

Song and calls: Call a short, metallic 'chup', which to a practised ear sounds clearer than the House Sparrow's.

Where and when: Despite its decline, still found in many parts of rural Britain, with strongholds in south-east and central England, East Anglia, parts of Wales, northern England and southern Scotland. Small numbers also found in eastern Ireland. Resident, present throughout the year. Most likely to visit gardens in rural areas during autumn and winter.

Habits: Much like its commoner cousin: a sociable bird, often seen in flocks. However, not as brash as the House Sparrow, and more wary of humans.

Feeding: Natural diet includes insects during the breeding season and seeds and grains for the rest of the year. May come to peanut feeders.

Breeding: Builds a loose cup-shaped nest, often in a hole in a tree or wall, occasionally in a hedge. Lays between four and six buffish eggs with dark spotting, which hatch 11–14 days later. Young fledge after 12–14 days. Two, sometimes three, broods.

CHAFFINCH

Fringilla coelebs

adult male summer

adult male winter

adult female summer

juvenile

adult female summer

Once Britain's commonest breeding bird, the Chaffinch is still very numerous, with more than seven million breeding pairs in Britain and Ireland. The male is one of our most handsome common birds, and always a welcome garden visitor.

Identification features: 15.5 cm (6 in). A large, slim finch, with striking white wingbars present in both sexes. The male has bright orange-pink face and underparts, a grey crown and nape, dark wings with a double white wingbar, and in flight a greenish-olive rump. The female is a more sombre version of the male, with mainly brown plumage and buffish underparts. Both have a sharp, cone-shaped bill for removing seeds from their food-plants.

Song and calls: Male's song a charming and distinctive arpeggio of notes, speeding up to end with a flourish. Also has a wide variety of calls, including the well-known 'pink' which is the origin of the name 'finch'.

Where and when: Common and widespread throughout Britain and Ireland, apart from a few remote islands or the highest mountain tops. Resident, though in winter numbers are boosted by immigrants from Continental Europe.

Habits: A confiding bird, often tamer than its relatives. Tends to feed in the open, often on lawns.

Feeding: Like many finches, feeds mainly on invertebrates during the breeding season, and seeds, grains and berries in autumn and winter. Will often feed on seeds and nuts spilled beneath a bird table.

Breeding: Builds a nest in the fork of a bush or tree, laying between three and five pale

blue eggs with dark spotting. The eggs hatch after 11–13 days, and the young fledge 12–15 days later. One or two broods.

BRAMBLING

Fringilla montifringilla

adult male winter
adult female winter
juvenile
adult female summer
adult male summer

A close relative of the Chaffinch, the Brambling is primarily an autumn and winter visitor to Britain and Ireland. Numbers vary considerably from year to year, depending on the availability of the species' favourite food, beech nuts. Bramblings often travel in mixed flocks with other finches and buntings, maximising their chances of finding food.
Identification features: 15.5 cm (6 in). The male Brambling is a handsome bird, with dark blackish head, rusty-orange breast, and dark back and wings, streaked with orange and white. The female is much duller, with a greyish-brown head and less bright orange in plumage. In flight reveals an obvious white rump (though beware confusion with Bullfinch, which also shows this feature).
Song and calls: The Brambling's best-known calls are a soft 'juk-juk' and a harsher 'wee-eek' – a combination which has been described as 'chuckle and squeak'!
Where and when: A widely

scattered winter visitor to most parts of Britain, occurring in very variable numbers from year to year. Also found in Ireland, but scarce there. Flocks usually start to arrive in early autumn and leave by late March or April. May visit gardens in rural areas, usually in the company of Chaffinches.
Habits: In winter, generally found in mixed flocks with other finches, sparrows and buntings.
Feeding: In winter feeds almost exclusively on seeds, with a special preference for beech-

mast. Will also take seeds from feeding-stations, often hopping about beneath to collect the spilled food.
Breeding: Brambling is a very rare breeder in Britain, with only a handful of pairs nesting each year.

GREENFINCH

Carduelis chloris

adult male summer
adult female summer
juvenile
adult female summer

A popular garden bird, Greenfinches are the main rivals to Blue and Great Tits when it comes to peanut feeders. They are the commonest finch in gardens, often roosting and nesting as well as feeding there.
Identification features: 15 cm (6 in). As its name suggests, the Greenfinch has a mainly green plumage, offset by the pale bill, dark grey wings with yellow edges, and a dark grey tail. The male is considerably brighter than the female. Juveniles are much duller, sometimes virtually brown, with streaky underparts. In flight reveals yellow patches on the wings and sides of the tail.
Song and calls: Song a harsh, wheezy 'dszhwee', repeated at regular intervals, and often delivered from a high perch. Also gives a variety of twittering calls.
Where and when: Widespread throughout Britain, apart from parts of north-west Scotland and Shetland. Also found throughout Ireland. Especially

common in south-east England, where it can be found in most gardens. Resident, present throughout the year.
Habits: May be seen calling in flight or from a tall bush or tree, or feeding on a bird table or feeder.
Feeding: During the breeding season eats seeds and insects, while in autumn and winter feeds mainly on seeds and nuts.
Breeding: A colonial nester, building a large cup of grass in the fork of a tree or bush, often a thick conifer. Lays between

three and six pale eggs with dark spotting, which hatch after 12–14 days. The young fledge 13–17 days later. Two or three broods.

GOLDFINCH

Carduelis carduelis

adult

juvenile

adult

This charming and attractive finch was once trapped in huge numbers for the cagebird trade, though fortunately this practice has long since been outlawed. Goldfinches have a very specialised diet of weed seeds, so if you want to attract them you may have to sacrifice some of your garden to wilderness!

Identification features: 14 cm (5.5 in). A brightly-coloured, slender finch, with a bright red face, black and white head pattern, delicate buffish plumage, and black wings edged with the gold strip which gives the species its name. Sexes alike. Juveniles have a plain brown head and face. In flight, gold wings contrast with black.

Song and calls: A delightful, musical twittering, generally uttered in flight. Song an extended version of the call, including trills.

Where and when: Widespread throughout England, Wales and southern and central Scotland; scarce elsewhere. Thinly scattered throughout Ireland. Resident, present throughout the year, but more likely to visit gardens in autumn and winter.

Habits: Generally travels in small, noisy flocks. Often perch on plants in order to remove seeds from flower-heads.

Feeding: Uses its sharp, conical bill to remove seeds, especially those which other species find hard to extract, such as the teasel. Will also feed on insects while breeding.

Breeding: Builds a small, cu-shaped nest from grass lined with hair or feathers, often on the outermost twigs of a tree. Lays between four and six pale eggs with darker spotting and streaking, which hatch 12–14 days later. Young fledge after 12–15 days. Two or three broods.

REDPOLL

Carduelis flammea

adult male summer

adult male winter

adult female summer

juvenile

adult female summer

One of our less familiar finches, the Redpoll visits gardens far more rarely than its close relative the Siskin. Superficially dull brown in colour, closer views reveal the bright crimson patch on the forehead which gives the species its common name.

Identification features: 12–13 cm (4.5–5 in). A small, plump finch, with a dark streaky plumage and two faint buffish wingbars. The male has a prominent red patch on the front of his head, which is also present, though smaller and less noticeable, in the female. Juvenile lacks red on head, and

has few obvious identification features. In winter, flocks of British Redpolls may be joined by larger, paler birds from northern races, known as 'Mealy' Redpolls.

Song and calls: Often calls in flight, giving a characteristic series of staccato notes reminiscent of hitting the keys on a manual typewriter. Also gives a variety of trills and buzzing calls.

Where and when: As a breeding bird, main strongholds are Ireland, Scotland, and Wales, with smaller numbers in eastern England and the south-west. Often associated with scattered

wooded areas on moorland or heath. In winter more widespread in the south, though never a very regular visitor to gardens.

Habits: Generally travels in small flocks, often accompanied by Siskins, and usually given away by their calls. Generally shy, though may come to feeders in some rural areas.

Feeding: During the breeding season mainly feeds on insects, but in autumn and winter prefers seeds.

Breeding: Breeds mainly in birch or alder woodlands, and rarely does so in gardens. Lays four or five pale blue eggs

etched with darker markings, which hatch 10–14 days later. Young fledge after 11–14 days. One or two broods.

SISKIN

Carduelis spinus

adult male

adult female

adult female

juvenile

Once virtually confined to conifer woodlands, this attractive little finch has in recent years become a familiar garden visitor. It generally appears in flocks, often feeding on peanuts or seeds provided by humans.

Identification features: 12 cm (4.5 in). Our smallest regularly breeding finch, the Siskin superficially resembles a streaky, dark Greenfinch. Males have a black cap, greenish-yellow upperparts streaked with black, black wings with two yellow wingbars, a yellow breast and paler white belly, with a few black streaks. Females are duller, with no black on the head and less yellow in the plumage. Juvenile paler and streakier than female. In flight shows yellow rump.

Song and calls: Variety of rapid, chattering calls interspersed with Greenfinch-like wheezing.

Where and when: As a breeding bird mainly confined to coniferous woodlands in northern and western Britain, and a few parts of Ireland. In autumn, winter and early spring found far more extensively in southern Britain, often visiting gardens.

Habits: Generally travels in flocks, sometimes with other finches such as Redpolls. Has adapted well to garden feeding-stations, with a particular preference for peanuts in bags or wire feeders.

Feeding: Natural food includes seeds and insects, gleaned from trees. However, now seems to prefer peanuts!

Breeding: Breeds mainly in conifer plantations and woodlands, away from gardens. Lays between three and six pale bluish-white eggs, with a few spots, which hatch 11–14 days later. The young fledge after 13–15 days. Two broods.

LINNET

Carduelis cannabina

adult male summer

adult male winter

adult female summer

juvenile

adult female summer

Mainly a bird of farmland and heath, the Linnet forms large flocks in autumn and winter, which occasionally stray into gardens in search of food. Although dull brown outside the breeding season, the cock Linnet in breeding plumage is one of our most handsome small birds.

Identification features: 14 cm (5.5 in). The breeding male is unmistakable, with his buffish plumage offset by bright strawberry-red chest patches and forehead. Winter males, females and juveniles are duller brown, with variable dark streaking.

Song and calls: Light and melodious song led to the Linnet's popularity in Victorian times as a cagebird. Also gives a variety of twittering calls, generally uttered by the flock in flight.

Where and when: Along with many farmland birds, the Linnet has recently undergone a rapid decline in population and range. It is still a fairly common breeding bird in much of England and Wales and parts of southern and eastern Scotland. In Ireland the decline has been much more dramatic, and the species is now absent from many of its former haunts.

Habits: In autumn and winter generally forms flocks, sometimes with other finches, sparrows and buntings. May occasionally visit gardens, especially those near farmland.

Feeding: During the breeding season feeds mainly on insects, while in autumn and winter the diet changes to weed seeds.

Breeding: Builds a cup-shaped nest from grass, lined with feathers or hair, usually deep in

a thick bush. Lays between four and six pale eggs, covered with light scribble marks, which hatch after 10–14 days. Young fledge 11–13 days later. Two or three broods.

BULLFINCH

Pyrrhula pyrrhula

adult female

adult male

adult female

juvenile

Aptly-named, the Bullfinch has a huge head and stout bill which it uses to feed on the buds of fruit trees. Along with many farmland birds, its numbers have declined in recent years due to modern farming methods.
Identification features: 16 cm (6.5 in). With his bright cherry-red underparts, huge bill and black face and crown, the male Bullfinch is unmistakable. The female lacks the male's bright coloration, and is buffish-brown below. In flight, both sexes show a bright white rump contrasting with the dark back and wings. Juvenile resembles female but lacks black on face and head.
Song and calls: Characteristic call is a soft, piping 'piu', repeated at intervals.
Where and when: Despite its recent decline, still found widely throughout much of Britain and Ireland, though much scarcer in northern Britain, and absent from the Northern and Western Isles. Resident, present throughout the year.
Habits: A shy and surprisingly unobtrusive bird, often only seen briefly as it flies away when disturbed. In gardens, most likely to be seen feeding in bushes or trees.
Feeding: For much of the year feeds mainly on seeds, though in spring has a marked preference for the buds of fruit trees, to the annoyance of many farmers and market-gardeners.
Breeding: Builds a loose nest from twigs lined with grass and hair, usually deep inside a bush

or tree. Lays between three and six pale blue eggs finely spotted with black, which hatch after 12–14 days. Young fledge 15–17 days later. Two, occasionally three, broods.

HAWFINCH

Coccothraustes coccothraustes

adult male

adult female

juvenile

adult female

Our largest finch, the Hawfinch is a surprisingly shy bird, rarely seen well, if at all. Nevertheless, in some rural areas it is a regular visitor to gardens, where it can be watched cracking open seeds with its enormous and powerful bill.
Identification features: 18 cm (7 in). A very large finch, almost the size of a thrush, with a massive head and huge, conical bill giving it a top-heavy appearance. Plumage basically pale chestnut-brown, darker above and paler below, with a greyish collar, small black bib and black wings with a broad whitish wingbar. Female rather duller than male. In flight shows obvious pale bar along both top and bottom of the wing, with the dark wings contrasting with the paler body.
Song and calls: A very loud, almost explosive 'zik', generally uttered in flight, which is often the first clue to the bird's presence.
Where and when: Mainly found in suitable woodlands in south-east England and East Anglia, with a few scattered outposts in Wales, central and northern England and southern Scotland. Not found in Ireland. Resident, but very localised, generally in woods with hornbeams or cherry trees.
Habits: A very shy bird, which rarely visits gardens, except those in rural areas near suitable habitat.
Feeding: Feeds on seeds and berries, with a special preference for cherry stones and beech nuts.
Breeding: Builds a small cup-shaped nest out of twigs lined with fine material, usually on a branch of a tree in woodland. Does not normally nest in gardens. Lays four or five pale blue or white eggs with darker spotting, which hatch after 9–14 days. Young fledge 10–14 days later.

YELLOWHAMMER

Emberiza citrinella

adult male summer

adult male winter

adult female summer

juvenile

adult female summer

'Hammer' derives from a German word meaning 'little bird', so Yellowhammer means, quite simply, 'little yellow bird'! A member of the bunting family, it is mainly associated with farmland, though may occasionally visit gardens to feed, especially in hard winter weather.

Identification features: 16.5 cm (6.5 in). The adult male in breeding plumage has a bright lemon-yellow head with black markings, chestnut-brown upperparts heavily streaked with black, yellowish underparts, and chestnut sides to the breast. The female is much less brightly-coloured, with a brownish-yellow plumage and streaky underparts. Outside the breeding season the male more closely resembles the female. In flight shows a plain chestnut rump contrasting with the streaked wings.

Song and calls: Song the famous 'little-bit-of-bread-and-no-cheese', a rhythmic, accelerating series of notes with a final flourish.

Where and when: Once common and widespread throughout rural Britain and Ireland, apart from the far north and west, the Yellowhammer has, like many farmland species, undergone a rapid and serious decline in recent years, and is absent from many of its former haunts. Resident, but in autumn and winter often forms mixed feeding flocks with other buntings, finches and sparrows, and may visit gardens near suitable habitat.

Habits: Often perches on hedgerows, especially when singing. In autumn and winter, most likely to be seen feeding on the ground or perched in a low bush.

Feeding: During the breeding season feeds mainly on insects; in autumn and winter switches diet to seeds and berries.

Breeding: Breeds almost exclusively on farmland, away from gardens. Lays between three and five pale eggs with dark spots, which it incubates for 11–14 days. Young fledge 12–13 days later. Two or three broods.

REED BUNTING

Emberiza schoeniclus

adult male summer

adult male winter

adult female summer

juvenile

adult female summer

Once rare in gardens, in recent years this attractive little bunting has become an increasingly regular garden visitor, often in the company of other buntings, finches and sparrows. Like so many of our farmland breeding birds, it is currently undergoing a population decline.

Identification features: 15.5 cm (6 in). The male is a striking and handsome bird, with a black head, face and throat contrasting with a bright white collar and moustachial stripe. Upperparts rich brown, heavily streaked with black; underparts are greyish-white with a few fine black streaks. Female is much duller: superficially resembling a female House Sparrow, but with richer chestnut upperparts contrasting with greyish underparts, and a more heavily marked face-pattern.

Song and calls: Song is a monotonous, rather hesitant, series of notes, which to my ears sound rather like a sound engineer: 'One. Two. Three. Testing'.

Where and when: Despite its recent decline, still widespread across much of Britain and Ireland, though rare or absent from many upland areas. Often associated with marshy areas or farmland, though in autumn and winter will also visit gardens in search of food.

Habits: Generally seen in small groups with other seed-eating birds, foraging on the ground.

Feeding: Feeds mainly on seeds, and will also take food from feeding-stations.

Breeding: Breeds mainly in reed beds or farm crops, away from gardens. Lays four or five olive-buff eggs with dark spots and blotches, which hatch 12–14 days later. Young fledge after 10–13 days.

Useful Addresses

RSPB (ROYAL SOCIETY FOR THE PROTECTION OF BIRDS)
The Lodge, Sandy, Beds SG19 2DL
Tel: 01767 680551

- With more than a million members, the RSPB is Europe's leading bird conservation organisation.

- As well as campaigning for the welfare of birds in Britain and abroad, it runs over 100 bird reserves up and down the country.

- There is also a national network of members' groups where you can meet other members, attend talks and go on field trips.

- Members receive a quarterly magazine, *Birds*.

- The RSPB mail-order catalogue includes an excellent range of garden bird equipment, including bird tables, nestboxes, food and feeders.

- The RSPB runs an excellent enquiry service, answering questions on bird welfare from members of the public (open weekdays, 9.30am–5pm; telephone 01767 680551).

- The junior arm of the RSPB, for members up to the age of 16, is the YOC (Young Ornithologists Club), whose members receive a bi-monthly magazine, *Bird Life*, and have the opportunity to go on field trips and other activities up and down the country.

BTO (BRITISH TRUST FOR ORNITHOLOGY)
The Nunnery, Thetford, Norfolk IP24 2PU
Tel: 01842 750050

- The BTO is Britain's leading organisation for scientific research on birds, carrying out a wide range of surveys, most of which rely on the participation of amateur birdwatchers.

- Members receive a bi-monthly magazine, *BTO News*.

- The BTO's most popular survey is the Garden BirdWatch. More than 10,000 participants record daily records of birds visiting their garden, and receive discounts on bird food as well as a regular newsletter, *The Bird Table*.

- Other BTO surveys include the long-running Nest Record Scheme, for recording data on breeding birds.

WILDBIRD FOODS
The Rea, Upton Magna, Shrewsbury SY4 4UR
Tel: 01743 709420

- Britain's leading supplier of wild bird food and feeders, and sponsors of the BTO's Garden BirdWatch survey.

- Wildbird Foods produce a free illustrated catalogue, which contains excellent advice on attracting birds to your garden as well as a list of products for sale by mail order.

- Wildbird Foods provide a fast, helpful and reliable mail order service for books on birds and other aspects of natural history, including those on garden birds. Free catalogue available on request.

GARDEN BIRD SUPPLIES LTD.
Wem, Shrewsbury SY4 5BF
Tel: 01939 232233
www.gardenbird.com

- Garden bird feeding specialists offering a huge range of foods, feeders, nest boxes and accessories – all available by mail order. Their free, full-colour Garden Bird Feeding Guide contains all their products, as well as information, hints and tips on getting the most out of your garden bird feeding. RSPB Corporate Partner. BTO Business Ally. Birdcare Standards Association Member.

WILDSOUNDS
Dept GFB, Cross Street, Salthouse, Norfolk NR25 7XH
Tel: 01263 741100

- Wildsounds run a mail order service selling CDs and tapes of bird and other wildlife sounds, including several featuring garden birds. Free catalogue available on request.

Further Reading

BOOKS ON GARDEN BIRDS

■ *Attracting Birds to Your Garden* by Stephen Moss & David Cottridge (New Holland, £16.99)

■ *The Complete Garden Bird Book* by Mark Golley, Stephen Moss & David Daly (New Holland, £9.99)

■ *The Pocket Guide to Garden Birds* by Dominic Couzens & Mike Langman (Mitchell Beazley, £7.99)

■ *The RSPB Birdfeeder Handbook* by Robert Burton (Dorling Kindersley, £15.99)

OTHER BOOKS ON BIRDS

■ *Collins Bird Guide* by Lars Svensson, Peter Grant, Killian Mullarney & Dan Zetterstrom (HarperCollins, £25.00)

■ *The Pocket Guide to Birds of Britain and North-West Europe* by Chris Kightley, Steve Madge & Dave Nurney (Pica Press, £11.95)

■ *Bill Oddie's Birds of Britain and Ireland* by Bill Oddie (New Holland, £12.99)

■ *Collins Field Guide to Bird Songs and Calls* by Geoff Sample (HarperCollins, £19.99)

■ *Collins Wings Guide to British Birds* by Dominic Couzens (HarperCollins, £12.99)

MAGAZINES

■ *BBC Wildlife*
Available monthly from newsagents, or by subscription from:
BBC Wildlife Subscriptions, PO Box 425, Woking, Surrey GU21 1GP

■ *Birdwatch*
Available monthly from larger newsagents, or by subscription from:
Birdwatch (Subs Dept.), Fulham House, Goldsworth Road, Woking, Surrey GU21 1LY

■ *Birdwatching*
Available monthly from larger newsagents, or by subscription from:
Birdwatching subscriptions, Tower Publishing Services Ltd, Tower House, Sovereign Park, Market Harborough, Leics LE16 9EF

■ *British Birds*
Available monthly by subscription only from:
Erika Sharrock, Fountains, Park Lane, Blunham, Bedford MK44 3NJ. Tel/Fax: 01234 364366

Picture Credits

The copyright in the photographs in this book belongs to the following:

(t = top; b = bottom; l = left; r = right; c = centre; tl = top left; tr = top right; tc = top centre; bc = bottom centre; bl = bottom left; br = bottom right)

CJ Wildbird Foods
CJ Wildbird Foods: 61tr; Mike Read: 24, 56, 65, 71; Gareth Thomas: 20, 57bl, 60tc, 61tl, 67, 72; David White: 12bl, 12br, 16, 29bl, 54, 57tl, 57tr, 58t, 58b, 59, 60tl, 60tr, 62br, 63, 66t, 66b

Frank Lane Picture Agency
David Dalton: 70; David T. Grewock: 57br; Paul Hart: 68b; Jurgen Sohns: 69; Roger Wilmshurst: 73

Natural Image
Robin Fletcher: 77br, 86tl, 86bl, 88tl; Bob Gibbons: 17, 28, 33, 35, 37, 39, 49, 51, 53, 55, 61br, 62t, 68t, 74, 75, 76tl, 76tr (left), 76br (both), 77tl (both), 77tr, 76bl (both), 78tl, 78tr, 78bl, 78br, 79l, 79tr, 79br (both), 80tl, 80tr, 80b, 81bl, 81r, 82t, 82bl, 82br, 83tl, 83bl, 83r, 84tl, 84tr, 84bl, 85tl, 85tr, 85bl, 85br, 86tr, 86br, 87tr (both), 87b, 88tr, 88b, 89tl, 89tr, 89bl, 90tl, 90tr, 90bl, 90br, 91tl, 91tr, 91bl, 91br, 92tl (both), 92tr, 92bl, 92br, 93tl, 93tr, 93bl, 93br, 94tr, 94bl, 94br, 95tl, 95tr (both), 95bl, 96tl, 96tr, 96bl, 96br, 97tl, 97tr, 97bl, 97br, 98tl, 98tr, 98bl, 98br, 99tl, 99tr, 99bl, 99br, 100l, 100tr, 100br, 101tl, 101tr, 101bl, 101br; Liz Gibbons: 47, 76bl, 89br; Peter Wilson: 76tr (right), 81tl, 84br, 87tl, 94tl

Windrush Photos
David Tipling: 5t, 5b, 13, 21tl, 21r, 21bl, 25l, 25r, 29br, 34, 36, 40, 46, 50, 52, 102, 103

The publishers would like to thank all photographers for their kind permission to reproduce the photographs

Index

Entries in bold indicate a main directory entry